Airlie:
The Garden of Wilmington

What peace we can remember
is down at Airlie now
where peach is flowering and pear
is bright upon the bough -
where quietly upon the lake
the white swans and the black
glide, haughtily reflected,
down the sky and back.

by Susan Taylor Block

ISBN 0-9717112-0-8

Printed by Friesens, Inc.
Canada

Edited by Suzanne N. Ruffin
Cover photo by Jack Davis, digitally altered by Jane L. Baldridge
Cover and book design by Jane L. Baldridge
Page one excerpt from *The Swans of Airlie* by Ulrich Troubetzkoy
(First published in the Christian Science Monitor, 1943)

First Edition

This book is dedicated to Jane Pope Akers Ridgway.

Acknowledgments

Many people provided facts, insight, maps, papers and photos that helped piece together the story of Airlie Gardens. Complicated, like layers of jigsaw puzzles, the tale of the garden and its former inhabitants could fill several books. This first edition, created to coincide with the centennial celebration, is merely a brief history of a very old property.

Several people deserve special praise. I am indebted to Christine Leahy, a true lover of Airlie who infused others with her enthusiasm and did much to promote the idea of a bound volume. The late William M. Reaves, a tireless compiler of newspaper articles. located the majority of the local press reports cited here. Also, the late Eugene C. Hicks, a gifted local genealogist, helped by tracing the lines of many people who are connected to the Airlie story.

Beverly Tetterton and Joseph Sheppard, New Hanover County local history librarians, have gone far beyond their duties to provide little known references and images; Barbara Rowe, curator of Cape Fear Museum and the first coordinator of Airlie's history program; Timothy Bottoms of Cape Fear Museum; Diane Cobb Cashman, Dr. James Rush Beeler, Merle Chamberlain, Eli Naeher, and Zee Reitblatt, of the Lower Cape Fear Historical Society; Jan Brewington, Wrightsville Beach Museum, Sadie Hood, director of the Wilmington Railroad Museum, Will Molineux, a historian in Williamsburg, Virginia; Elizabeth Wilson, of the Hampton, Virginia Public Library; Michael Cobb, Hampton History Museum; Dr. Alan Watson, and W. Andrew Boney.

Two formidable researchers, William R. Johnston and Walter E. Campbell, Henry Walters's and William Rand Kenan's biographers, respectively, have contributed generously to what we know about the Jones-Walters world.

Jane Pope Akers Ridgway shared facts and impressions that augment this work.

Eleanor Wright Beane has been a tremendous resource. Her memories of Airlie, the Lodge and the neighborhood gave depth to printed descriptions and added many details that might one day have been lost.

Additional information came from: Rosalie Watters Carr, Peter Browne Ruffin, Stewart Barney Kean, George Evans, Elsie Corbett Hatch, Fred Hatch, Harold Alfonzo Franks, James Lofton, William Dobo, Daniel deButts, Lossie Gardell, Elaine Henson, George Evans, Jr., Norris Evans, Gary Evans, Rodney Evans, Barbara Marcroft, Bill Creasy, Mary McCarl Wilson, Isabel James Lehto, Kathryn London Stirk, John J. Burney, Jr., Bonnie R. Burney, Louis A. Burney, Jr., Kenneth Davis, Mr. and Mrs. Luther T. Rogers, Janet K. Seapker, Jane Holman Hardwick, Agnes Rankin Beane, Juanita Lacewell, Ruby Rogers McGowan, Nicki Yow, Donald D. Getz and Tom Ridgway.

I am thankful to: Allan T. Strange, Ann Hewlett Hutteman, Dave Carnell, Edward F. Turberg, Henry B. Rehder, Catherine Stribling, Donna Lux, Albert Corbett, J. W. Taylor, Jr., Jan Costly, Alyce Dana, Jeffery Flack, Joanne Fogler, Leslie N. Boney, Sue Boney Ives, Sandra Corbett Hiatt, Bobby Jones, Frances S. Moffitt, Marguerite Powell, Carole C. Reynolds, Taylor Cromartie, Anna Pennington, Betty Hill Taylor, and Mary Wilson; also the late Bishop Thomas H. Wright, Carl McGowan, Georgie Franks, Maxine Dizor, and Bishop Hunley Elebash.

It was, again, a great pleasure to work with book designer and artist Jane Baldridge and editor Suzanne Ruffin.

My husband, Frederick L. Block, has, as always, been my greatest encouragement.

Airlie Road, about 1890 (Margaret Moore Perdew)

Governor's Point

"To spend a quiet season, free from the cares and worries of our work-day life, and to breathe with never-ending delight, the life-giving breezes which flow from the bosom of the ocean."
William Latimer, June 16, 1888, at the dedication of the Seacoast Railway.

When we celebrate the beauty of Airlie Gardens, we remember primarily the interesting, dynamic woman who envisioned and executed the botanical wonderland: Sarah Jones Walters. A fascinating character, she dazzled and fascinated even the most reticent, yet retained a sense of wonder for nature's simplest delights. Though fortune and affiliations afforded her entree to America's most privileged society, she stayed true to the spirited yet sensitive Southern girl she always was, and the gardens she created mirror her nature: native and entrancing.

But Sarah Walters was not the first person to see the potential of the land. By virtue of simple geography it was always prime property. Native Americans inhabited the jutting peninsulas, eating hickory nuts and harvesting oysters, crabs, clams, and shrimp from the crystal waters. They enjoyed the natural theater of clouds, moonlight, and sunrises from geographical front-row seats, but if autumn storms caused the waters to rise, there was plenty of high ground for sanctuary. The natives themselves added to the beauty of the landscape. John Lawson observed coastal Carolina Indians in the early 18th century and wrote: "Their gait (is) sedate and majestic. They are dexterous and steady, both as to their hands and feet, to admiration. They will walk over deep brooks and creeks on the smallest poles, and without any fear or concern."[1]

Native Americans (N.C. Division of Archives & History.)

Native Americans considered nature, including waterfront property, beyond human ownership. However, European settlers arrived in the 1730s with long held ideas to the contrary. Promises of land, registered in duly recorded deeds, lured waves of immigrants from Scotland, Ireland, Wales, Germany, and Switzerland to North Carolina. Royal Governor Gabriel Johnston (1699-1752), a Scots lowlander and former professor of Oriental languages at St. Andrews University, signed numerous land grants that deeded abundant acreage to adventurous souls willing to sacrifice convenience for opportunity. Gov. Johnston used his influence to move the center of local government and commerce from Brunswick Town, on the west side of the Cape Fear River, to Newton, on the opposite side. Then, in 1739/40, he changed the city's name to one that would honor the British politician who had nominated him for the office of governor: Spencer Compton, Earl of Wilmington. Compton, who jockeyed for power against Robert Walpole, served as chief minister of England, in 1742-43.

On February 20, 1735, King George II granted, through Governor Johnston, a 640-acre tract of land to Solomon and Jonathan Ogden. Solomon Ogden was a carpenter; Jonathan, a cordwainer. Both lived in Newton, renamed Wilmington, in 1739/40. With both impermanent and watery boundaries, the property must have been the stuff of nightmares for subsequent surveyors, for the land ran from "the mouth of the Creek where it falls into the Sound" to a "Hickory saplin" to a "Gum," then down the "Creek to the first Station." The creek, known then as Lee's or Grainger's Creek, is now called Bradley Creek, and a portion of the original Ogden grant is known to us today as Airlie.

Back then, there was one startling difference in the neighborhood. Deep Inlet, which existed until at least 1858, cut through what is now known as Wrightsville Beach almost due east of the Airlie land and aligned with Bradley Creek. It was such a dominant feature that the Ogdens called the tract "Deep Inlet on the Sound." Waves breaking on the shore created an audio backdrop, both outdoors and indoors, that ranged from enchanting lull to frightening roar. Deep Inlet also added to the allure of the land: easy access to the Atlantic Ocean. A hurricane closed Deep Inlet, once located near the Carolina Yacht Club.[2]

Two years later, the Ogden brothers deeded half the tract to Thomas Clark, a Wilmington merchant whose children were Col. Thomas Clark, an officer in the Revolutionary War, and Ann Clark Hooper, wife of William Hooper, a signer of the Declaration of Independence. In 1738, when Clark sold the 320-acre tract to Gabriel Johnston (1699-1752), the land acquired a new name: "Governor's Point." Gabriel Johnston, North Carolina's second Royal

Governor, had been a university professor before tackling the job of governing the rugged province. He built a modest soundfront home and named a small island off the southeast corner of his property "The Enjoyment," but probably spent little time at either. His demanding job required much travel and paid little. But his ties to the crown made him the most prominent member of the "old boys' network," and his payoff was in land, a currency still held in abundance.[3]

"All the rest of our time is spent at our own little plantations which are some fifty, some a hundred, and some two hundred miles distant from one another," he wrote, in 1746. Governor's Point had the edge on naming: Johnston also owned Conehoe, a silkworm farm in Tyrrell County, and Possum Quarter in Granville County. At his death, in 1752, he was truly "land-poor," owning about 35,000 acres of Carolina turf, but little cash: His salary was 14 years in arrears. When Governor Johnston's widow, Frances, married John Rutherford, "Receiver General of his Majesty's Quit Rent for the Province of N. C.," he took control of Governor's Point.[4]

A subsequent owner, Alexander Duncan, was a shipping business partner of Robert Schaw and John Ancrum. In 1775, he "shot himself in the head with a pistol."

Wrightsville

Governor's Point went through a series of sales until the year 1800, when Judge Joshua Grainger Wright purchased it for £110. Col. Thomas Wright, Judge Wright's brother, handled the estate sale in his official capacity as High Sheriff of New Hanover County. The brothers were great-grandsons of Wilmington co-founder Joshua Grainger and sons of wealthy privateer and Wrightsboro planter Captain Thomas Wright (1714-1771). The younger brother, Joshua G. Wright, was a respected attorney and Speaker of the N. C. General Assembly. His wife, Susan Bradley Wright, was the daughter of Richard and Elizabeth Sharpless Bradley, devout Quakers who had made sure their daughter had more than a passing knowledge of the Bible. Going against the social trend of the day, they may have been less than pleased that their daughter was marrying a member of St. James Church, but at least they could console themselves that the groom's maternal side, the Joshua Grainger family, had also been Quakers.[5]

The two young people had been neighbors in what they simply called Wilmington and what is now known as the Historic District. Joshua Grainger Wright lived on the southwest corner of Third and Market streets in an elegant home that his father, Captain Thomas Wright, had leased and put under a verbal offer-to-purchase contract with owner John Burgwin. In 1799, the son would make good on the offer when he bought the house for 3500 Spanish milled dollars. Susan Bradley lived on South Second Street between Ann and Nun streets.

As a unique bond, both Susan Bradley and Joshua Wright had seen their respective houses occupied by British officers during the American Revolution. When General Cornwallis moved Major Craig out of the Burgwin-Wright house, Craig took over the Bradleys' home. On Wrightsville Sound, the two families became neighbors as well. In 1808, Joshua Grainger Wright sold his brother-in-law, Richard Bradley, approximately one-fifth of the tract, sixty-five acres of land "on the creek," for five shillings. Although the creek would continue to be called Lee's Creek, at least until 1855, the name soon after was changed to Bradley's Creek. The Bradleys sold part of their land to Henry Savage, Zebulon Latimer and others. By the time the Bradley parcel became part of Airlie, it had been whittled down to 25 acres, enormous by today's standards, but a typical soundfront lot at that time.

The land Joshua Wright purchased was still wilderness. Just beyond the bald shore, it was raw and rife with wildlife. Panthers the size of large greyhounds and the color of lions crouched in live oak limbs waiting to snatch a hunk of rump from an unsuspecting deer. Bear, hunted for their analgesic oil, were known to tear the coat off hunting dogs, leaving some of their prey alive but clothed only in pink glistening flesh. Rattlesnakes devoured small prey silently, but shook their inimitable instruments when they encountered creatures too big to pass through their unhinged jaws. Another snake, the water moccasin, was prevalent in swamps and ponds. It had a "prodigious wide Mouth" and was "mottled and very poisonous." It did not grow to be very long, but was "the Thickness of the Calf of a Man's Leg."[6]

Nevertheless, the Wrights decided to build a summer home on the sound, both for a change of scenery and to escape the staggering heat of Wilmington summers. Space, breeze, and salt baths were considered good medicine, and many seasonal Sound residents did not return to town until the first frost. Judge Wright, though only 32 when he purchased the land, had already lost three children to illness. He himself suffered from some unspecified malady and would live only to the age of 43.[7]

Though slightly different versions of the naming of Mount Lebanon exist among Wright family papers, the one remembered by Judge Wright's granddaughter, Ann Eliza Meares, might be closest to the truth. Shortly after he purchased the property, Susan and Joshua Wright were riding horses on their newly acquired soundfront estate. There were cedar trees all around them, a wood considered soft in America but prime building material in the Middle East. Susan Bradley was familiar with Old Testament history in which the mammoth cedars from Mount Lebanon were floated down the water toward Jerusalem for the construction of Solomon's temple.

So, according to the cherished tradition, with a gentle touch to her pony, she rode forward to an eminence, near which stood large cedar trees and said, "We will build here and call our home Mount Lebanon." It is interesting that she chose not to incorporate the name "Wright," leaving it to others to name waterfront locales after her husband's family.[8]

Place names change, not only through new ownership but by being altered with use. Just as Bradley's Creek has been recently whittled down to the nonpossessive form, the name Susan Bradley chose has been "dismounted" on and off for at least 201 years. Her own husband used "Lebanon, near Wilmington" as his return address, but their son, Dr. Thomas Henry Wright, preferred "Mount Lebanon." After the Herbert Latimer family purchased the eastern portion of Dr. Wright's tract, in 1886, they called it Lebanon. Pembroke Jones, after purchasing a large portion of Mount Lebanon, referred to the land's past as "the old Wright farm." Before the name Wright took hold, the Sound was also known as New Topsail and Summer Ville.[9]

Additionally, the entire neighborhood was called "Wrightsville," a tradition that continued until at least 1906, long after the settlement of the adjacent beach required the new longer labelings, Wrightsville Sound and Wrightsville Beach.[10]

On a prominence at Mount Lebanon, "immediately on the Sound," Susan Bradley and Joshua Wright built a two-story frame house with a full basement. The summer home had six fireplaces, though seldom were they necessary. Insurance documents state that each story measured 40' by 20'. The dimensions seem small for such a large family: the Wrights had thirteen children, eight of whom survived childhood. But there was little more room in their town home: The Burgwin-Wright house measured about 50' by 25' before the 19th-century addition. However, both houses were augmented by outbuildings. The 1600-square-foot house at Mount Lebanon had an attached storage room, a detached kitchen 60' east of the house and a lumber room.[11]

Mount Lebanon, 1958 (Lower Cape Fear Hisorical Society)

Sleeping porches provided even more space. They were popular not only because one could take advantage of the nighttime breeze, but because fresh air was considered prophylactic therapy for many diseases, especially tuberculosis. The most comfortable sleeping porches were upstairs, where the breeze would be the best air conditioner available.

The aesthetic atmosphere was far different from a climate controlled boudoir: sometimes more pleasant, sometime unbearable. Cricket serenades, the sound of breaking waves borne on the east wind, and the occasional poetic toll of a sea buoy wafted through, providing audio backdrop scarcely noticed by those accustomed to it. When frogs broke into their loud, uncouth croaks, children giggled late at night as they played a game of guessing what the frogs might be trying to say. But on occasion the breeze stilled, quiet reigned, and heat, humidity and surreptitious insects known locally as "no-see-ums" made the term "sleeping porches" a misnomer.[12]

By at least 1815, the entire area had become known as Wrightsville. John Willkings, a relative of the Wrights, posted this ad in the *Wilmington Gazette* on April 27 of that year. "For sale: Liberal Terms. That healthy Summer residence at Wrightsville on the Sound belonging to the subscriber. There are about 20 acres of land with a comfortable house and out houses upon it. A garden with fruit trees and grape vines of various kinds, will add pleasure to the health which its situation offers. To a person desirous of entering into Salt business it furnishes an excellent stand for the erection of Works."[13]

Wrightsville Sound became known quickly for its hospitality. Homeowners generally welcomed house guests in droves and, usually, visitors came to stay a while: two to three weeks was not unusual. Just around the waterfront "corner," on Greenville Sound, Mary Bradley Green entertained so frequently at Shandy Hall that her son-in-law wrote, in 1825, "It is as impossible for her to live without a round of company as for a fish to exist out of water."[14]

Outbuildings at Mount Lebanon (Lower Cape Fear Historical Society)

The production and preparation of food and drink was time-consuming. In a day when there were no grocery stores and in a place far from the City Market at Front and Market streets, produce and meat had to be raised and bred. Most Soundfront residences were enclosed by white wooden fences designed to mark boundaries and contain farm animals. Chickens, roosters, cows, goats, pigs, mules and workhorses were all part of the noisy scene. Corncribs had to be checked regularly to ensure that the animals had enough food in store. Vegetable gardens were standard and required almost daily maintenance.

Pork, the courier of more flavor per pound than any other meat, was one of the most popular entrees at Wrightsville Sound. It was a vehicle for neighborhood hospitality as well. The Giles and Bradley families enjoyed giving each other pieces of warm, freshly cooked pork. "Your Pa had the hog killed the morning after he arrived," wrote Almeria Reston Giles to her son, Norwood, about 1861, "and James killed theirs the evening before, so we did not have the pleasure of sending a piece of pork to each other as we would if the killing took place at different times."[15]

Though the sound boasted some teetotalers, brandy, homemade wine, ale, rum, and a concoction called grog were common beverages. Judge Joshua Wright wrote from Lebanon, in 1810, "I have sent a keg of what is deemed by connoisseurs as well as amateurs, most excellent rum. All that I can say myself on the subject is that it has been more than eight years in my cellar and was at the time I purchased it reported to be two or three years old."

Of all Judge Wright's children, only one, the eldest son, would spend his whole life residing at Mount Lebanon in the summer and at the Burgwin-Wright House the remainder of the year. Although Wrights had occupied the house since the American Revolution, the property was not transferred until 1799, when Joshua Grainger Wright purchased it for 3500 Spanish milled dollars, or "pieces of eight." Dr. Thomas Henry Wright (1800-1861), who as the eldest son inherited both houses, was a physician, president of the Bank of Cape Fear, a director of the Wilmington and Weldon Railroad, the co-founder of the Seamen's Hospital, a merchant, a lauded Thalian performer adept at female impersonations and a frustrated architect. He married an "heiress," Mary Allan, and together they had eleven children.

Dr. Wright was also deeply religious, perhaps by nature alone, but certainly not discouraged by his mother who, long before the days of government assistance, was a sort of one-woman faith-based charity. Often needy people begged for food at her home on the sound, in summer, and the Burgwin-Wright House the remainder of the year. Her generosity continued throughout her life, despite the fact that she found what some beggars need is a large dose of honesty. A man purporting to be a deaf mute knocked on the townhouse door, as he had done twice a week for months. Susan Bradley Wright always felt particularly sorry for the speechless fellow and presented him with a generous cut of freshly cooked meat. When she handed him his ration he took one look at it and screamed, "Dammit woman, pork again!"[16]

Susan Bradley Wright
(Lower Cape Fear Historical Society)

Among Dr. Wright's male relations, making church history was a common thing. His first cousin, the Rev. Thomas Wright (1785-1835), performed the first Episcopal service in Chapel Hill, in 1820, and founded Calvary Protestant Episcopal Church in Memphis, in 1832. Dr. Wright's brother-in-law, the Rev. Adam Empie, was chaplain at West Point from 1814-1816, president of the College of William and Mary from 1827-1836, and founded the Army Chaplain's Corps. Another relation, William Mercer Green, organized the Episcopal congregation in Chapel Hill that came to be known as Chapel of the Cross. In 1842, the Rev. Green most likely procured the architect Thomas U. Walter, whose design for St. James Church in Wilmington had already become a recent reality. William Mercer Green was elected the first Episcopal Bishop of Tennessee, in 1849.[17]

Dr. Thomas Henry Wright shaped the face of local churches more than any other individual in Wilmington's history. He started tinkering in 1831, when he personally hired architect James F. Post to alter the pulpit of the original St. James Church building. In 1839, as St. James's senior warden, he dominated the building process of the new edifice. In 1851-53, he was instrumental in the construction of St. John's Church (now destroyed) at Third and Red Cross streets. But it was in 1835 that Dr. Wright made his sweetest contribution to local church life.

Our Little Chapel

by Claude Wingate, then of New Orleans -1858

Like a swan-white dove it nestles
In among the trees
Where every leaf at springtime rustles
In the passing breeze.
Rustic benches are around it
Carved with many a name
Here our fathers sat and rested
Here we do the same.
Here we sit and hear the Ocean
In the distant roar
See the white waves leaping upwards
High above the shore,
See the sunlight on the water
Glittering like a glow
While the old oaks bend o'er to meet it
Moss-clad they and hoary
Here a little bridge hath spanned it
Frail and weak it seemeth
Often have I love to stand when
Moonlight o'er it gleameth
Listening to chirp of katydids
That sing in the young elms
Letting my fancy wander free and
Picture distant realms
Musing upon the dead who lie
Asleep within those graves
Or dreaming o'er those wavelets free
About old Ocean's caves
Wondering what lovers here have sat
In sight of Church and Ocean
Plighting fond vows or silent stood
Entranced in deep emotion
But most I loved this spot when autumn
Storms have swept the grove
When brown June tassels strew the forest
Then I love to rove
Where hickory nuts come dropping 'round me
With sudden startling sound
And where the large and heavy raindrops
Have dimpled all the ground
And where the dry and broken twigs
Are scattered all around
Ere the wind has ceased to flutter
'Mongst the rustling trees
Playing wild mad pranks about me
With the withered leaves
Tossing hair and dress and apron
All about with ease
Till I draw my mantle closer
And run before the breeze
Now in fancy can I wander in the grove
See the bridge, the river
Every spot I love
That its image is not dimmed
Let this picture prove.

"In a secluded corner, almost hidden under a veil of moss, a little white chapel, where it ought to be easy to worship God. Behind it is a brick-walled burying ground, where one might rest in peace with the birds to sing a requiem." Susan Iden, 1936. (Susan Block)

Mount Lebanon Chapel

Mount Lebanon Chapel was born of faith and convenience. Though possible to travel to Wilmington for Sunday morning services, it was difficult. The road taken, now known as Wrightsville Avenue, was merely a bumpy dirt path in the 1830s. Planking and shelling would come later. The time span of the nine-mile journey was dependent upon weather, the horses' health and mood, and the buggy or carriage's condition. Typically, it could take as little as one frenzied hour or as much as three tiring hours.[18]

Some Wrightsville Sound families, like the Gileses, chose to conduct worship services at home. The Giles property, now home to Katherine Rhett and Judge James Fox, is on the north side of Bradley Creek, close to Airlie. The Foxes' home, Edge Hill, was reconstructed using materials from the original house that was occupied for almost a hundred years by the Gileses. Their landmark sailboat, *Vixen* (i. e., the female fox), marks the spot.

William B. Giles, who married a Wrightsville Sound resident, Annabella Fleeming, in 1804, purchased 20 1/2 acres on the creek for $899, from Benjamin Jacobs the following year. The Giles property was bordered on the west by the Restons' land, Honolulu, and on the east by a portion of Joshua G. Wright's 320-acre parcel, the adjacent 65-acre portion soon deeded to Richard Bradley. Prior to the construction of Mount Lebanon Chapel, in 1835, when the Gileses were in residence, "an Episcopal service was held in the house each Sunday. No work of any kind was allowed to be done by anyone, including the servants, on the Sabbath, and all cooking for Sunday had to be done on Saturday," wrote descendant Harriet Bellamy Jewett in 1964.[19]

In 1835, Dr. Thomas Henry Wright, who inherited 57 acres of his father's Mount Lebanon estate, decided to

Dr. Thomas Henry Wright (Lower Cape Fear Historical Society)

take matters into his own smooth hands. In his own words, he "presented" a 6.5-acre tract, with water access, to "St. James Church for the purpose of creating an Episcopal house of worship on Wrightsville Sound." The waterfront parcel allowed easy access for sound neighbors who could row or pole their boats to church. Dr. Wright requested it be named Mount Lebanon for his "country seat of which this tract forms a part."

Though other individuals contributed to the construction, it was primarily Dr. Wright who financed the project. It called for a vernacular rural chapel with smooth plaster walls, wooden pegs, wide-board heart pine floors, jewel-like casement windows and a chapel bell. Clean line pine benches surrounded the building and a little bridge spanned a nearby creek that no longer exists. The elegant simplicity of it all would have pleased even Dr. Wright's in-laws. The contractor, Hillary Bryant, must have worked fast, for a few months later, on the tricentennial of the printing of Coverdale's Bible, the first service was held at Mount Lebanon Chapel. Officiating was the Rev. Cameron Farquhar MacRae, a descendant of Alexander MacRae of Wilmington and the son-in-law of the Wrights' old friend, John Fanning Burgwin.[20]

By 1836, regular services were being held in the chapel, led alternately by Dr. Wright and James S. Green, a relative who also served as a lay reader at St. James Church. In June of that year, the Rev. Dr. Robert B. Drane of St. James Church administered the first Holy Communion at the chapel and performed the first baptism in the chapel. The baby was the fifth of Dr. Wright's children: James Allan Wright.[21]

The architectural style of Mount Lebanon Chapel is classified as Greco-Gothic and the National Register of Historic Places considers it a "robust example." The Greek portion speaks of the building's classical influence and is illustrated in its symmetry and stepped cornices. Although Gothic overtones are apparent in the pointed arches over each window, the label is not without irony. In true Gothic architecture, various other features shut the world out and force the worshipers' attention upward beyond the vaulted ceilings. The wall openings are full of inspirational and instructive stained glass that colors the light and hides whatever lies beyond them.

The irony lies in the fact that the worship experience in Lebanon Chapel is anything but vertical. It is as horizontal as the short board of the cross. Early on a dewy summer morning, with all the leaded windows flung open, the surrounding creation seems to become part of the building and usually as much a worship aid as a vaulted ceiling. Prior to the closing of Deep Inlet, due east of Lebanon, participants in the service could hear ocean waves breaking in the distance. Refreshing salty breezes, shimmering green leaves and the songs of birds remind the habitues as well as visitors to Mount Lebanon Chapel that the Spirit of the Creator is present.

But for Chapel worshipers who occasionally feel their attention running far afield, there is comfort in the experience of others. Tales abound, some almost Disneyesque, of the distractions of Mount Lebanon. The late Maxine Dizor once reminisced about a service there, in the late 1970s, made special by the presence of the Bishop. Somber expressions soon changed however to nervous jitters as a bird just outside one of the windows began to chirp in response to every statement made by the local minister. The effect was heightened because the bird sat silent as a stone each time the Bishop spoke. Additionally, more than one Wilmingtonian remembers a raccoon who used to poke its head out from the hollow of a tree every time the congregation responded in unison.[22]

But perhaps the most charming illustration of the distractions of Mount Lebanon comes from an 1895 account written by Dr. Wright's granddaughter, Caroline Green Meares. At that time, some of those who attended the chapel traveled on the shell-topped roads, but many came by boat, often poling their way across the marsh. Mrs. Meares's handwritten account testifies to how seamlessly the geography of the chapel moved her thoughts from religion to regatta and back again. "Memories cluster thick and strong around this little chapel, where the old residents would meet for worship, in flowered organdies and embroidered waistcoats, and after the little organ would peal its cracked 'Amen,' would gather for the social hour. Neighborly chats were held over the backs of pews — parties planned and the coming boat races discussed beneath the shadows of those towering oaks (veritable monarchs of the forest that had shaded and sheltered our illustrious fore-fathers in the centuries past as refuge from storm and sun).

"For Wrightsville held the honor of having one of the oldest boat racing clubs in the U. S. In fact, it was the second oldest boat racing club in the country, the New York Yacht Club holding the honor of the first and oldest in the country. But even this fact did not tempt them from the paths of duty: NEVER SAILING ON THE SABBATH.

"God's day was revered and after the return home, collects and hymns were learned and sung. Sweet were those days! Precious are those memories!"[23]

By the time these words were written, many changes had taken place in the Wright family and in the area surrounding Mount Lebanon. Four years after the completion of Mount Lebanon Chapel, a new building was erected for St. James Church. Rector Robert Drane praised Dr. Wright for the scope of his role in the creation of the 1839 Gothic-Revival style St. James building: "It is no exaggeration to say that but for his wise counsels, his munificence, his untiring energy and perseverance,....the edifice which is erected would never have been reared."

From the time of St. James's completion until Dr. Wright's death, he had 22 years to sit on his porch and watch the handsome tower clock measure the passing of time. Originally, ten additional finials, like the four that still adorn the tower, lined St. James Church. From Dr. Wright's vantage point, it must have been an awesome and inspiring view. But every summer, he continued to switch his attention to the little chapel when he left the heat of Third and Market for the modest air conditioning that his house in the cedar grove afforded.[24]

In 1839, the Church was struck by lightning, Dr. Wright wrote of the chapel. "The fluid appeared to have come from earth, dividing the pillar which supports the South East corner of the building into several parts, and then ascending and splitting the corner post and carried by the cornice to a hickory tree which stands within two or three feet of the building: - no other damage was sustained.

"In 1841, a small house occupied by a small family by the name of Armstrong, and situated near the residence of Mrs. Giles was struck by lightning. The only son, aged seventeen years, was struck dead, the father so severely burnt that he died the next week. One of their daughters was slightly burned, a horse and hog killed, and the chimney and part of the house shattered.

"The bodies of the deceased were deposited on the hill south of the church. This was the first interment made in that graveyard."[25]

Though Mount Lebanon Cemetery was vacant until 1841, two other cemeteries nearby were not. At Sedge Field, north of Lebanon, but south of what is now Oleander Drive, on Bradley Creek, there already existed a half-acre cemetery. Also, across Oleander, there was a family graveyard at Honolulu, the Restons' summer home, that is now a subdivision known as Bar Harbor. Eventually so many members of the Giles family were buried at Mount Lebanon that some Sound residents called it the "Giles Cemetery." However, from 1884-1910, eleven members of the Giles family were disinterred and reburied at Oakdale.[26]

Additionally, a single white marble grave at Airlie, apart from Mount Lebanon, is a site of titillating mystery. Bearing the inscription,"Known in Eternity. J. H," the monument marks the grave of a mysterious Frenchman who appeared in Wilmington in the 1840s. Though the grave bears a simple beauty, using mere initials juxtaposed with an entire phrase indicates the insignificance of the letters "J. H." According to local legend, "John Hill" was actually Marshal Ney, one of Napoleon's twelve generals. Erudite and eloquent, he tutored the children of Thomas and William Wright and Richard Bradley. He lived with the Bradley family and spent a lot of time sitting under the oaks with neighbors, in the very spot where he is buried. Though silent during his lifetime concerning his life in France, after his death, unsubstantiated rumors spread that a paper discovered among his personal effects bore the words, "I am the Marshal."

Wilmington historian Louis T. Moore (1885-1961) spoke well when he said that the stranger's "burial was made in a beautiful wooded dell. Here, for all time the sighing of the wind in the stately nearby trees will chant a never ending requiem for the soul of the dead unknown, sleeping in a friendly land far distant from his native home."

It is unknown whether the stranger acquired his name before or after he reached Wrightsville Sound, but it would have fit in perfectly. Judge Joshua Wright's niece, Ann Grainger Claypoole, married William Henry Hill, about 1810. Eliza R. Bradley, daughter of Richard Bradley (1769-1833), married Dr. John Hill in 1817 and William A. Wright wed his first cousin, Eliza Ann Hill, in 1830. This family of Hills descended from William Hill, a Harvard graduate who moved to Brunswick County in 1756, and then to New Hanover County when they purchased the Wrights' Wrightsboro plantation, Nesses Creek, or Fairfields, later renamed Hilton. Several members of the Hill family were buried at Mount Lebanon Cemetery, inside a handsome iron fence that still exists.

Actually "John Hill" wasn't the only refined 19th-century Frenchman to seek a new life in North Carolina. The story seems to mimic the tale of Peter Ney, a Frenchman who settled in Rowan County and declared, on his deathbed, "I am the Marshal." It is also reminiscent of the life of Alexander Calizance Miller, another well-educated Frenchman with an assumed name who moved to Wilmington in the early 1800s. Ironically, in 1811, Mr. Miller married Mary Brown, the daughter of Susan Bradley Wright's oldest sister, Lucy Bradley.[27]

John Hill's grave was known to Sarah Jones Walters. When she launched her mammoth landscaping venture, Hill's grave was the site of the first azalea planting. By the mid-1950s, that first plant had grown to be nine feet tall.

Transportation to the Sound changed in 1853 when the dirt road from downtown Wilmington was modernized. Known now as Wrightsville Avenue, the ancient road still follows the lines of the original byway. Wrightsville Sound residents welcomed the new wooden road for convenience's sake, but were wary of sightseers and increased development. Willie Giles echoed the concerns of his family and neighbors when he learned of the project: "The building of a plank-road as suggested is not a bad idea, but if all sorts of people are to come to the Sound to destroy the quiet and privacy of the place, I hope it will never even be begun."

Despite their uneasiness, the plank road, sometimes called a corduroy road, from the Sound into Wilmington opened November 15, 1853. Residents who lived along the road nicknamed it "Log Roll Road," a name that endured until recent years according to Lossie Gardell, who grew up in the area. "It has been passed down through my family that also there were 'rolly logs' across a shallow portion of Bradley Creek, and it could be crossed by foot."

Recreational transportation also changed at Wrightsville in 1853. Many residents of the Sound sailed competitively. Most of them were young men who engaged frequently in good-natured arguments about whose yacht was the swiftest. Norwood Giles joked, years later, that "the violence of the gesticulation, serves admirably to keep off sand flies." On April 24, Richard Bradley, Daniel Baker, Parker Quince, John Reston, Richard J. Jones, Talcott Burr and T. M. Gardner founded the Carolina Yacht Club. Richard Bradley was elected its first Commodore.

Soon, Roger Moore, William Wright, Oscar Parsley and John Quince joined. The boats' names were well-known in the area. Thomas Wright purchased the *Rob/Roy*; John Quince had the *Twilight*; Richard Bradley, *La Favorite*; and Henry Bradley owned the *Eliza Ann*. Competition did not change, nor did the "sunfish tales." However, club secretaries and pursers began keeping records, chronicling Wrightsville's great yachts and the people who captained them.[28]

The founding of Carolina Yacht Club also spawned more parties. Known originally as "bank parties," they took place on the strand on moonlit nights. Norwood Giles, in his 1886 history of the club, noted the strange patterns of footprints made after a young couple wandered out of sight, down the beach. "No wonder the present generation of sand crabs have prominent eyes when we consider the astonishment experienced by their ancestors at such carrying on."[29]

"The genial breezes dimpling our waters and the whiz of soda fountains jointly announce the arrival of that season when all true yachtsmen launch their hopes," wrote Pembroke Jones's business partner and frequent shipmate, Norwood Giles, in 1886. Pictured is a Carolina Yacht Club regatta, about 1925. Photo by Louis T. Moore (New Hanover County Public Library)

Less than Civil Times

Fun and frivolity gave way quickly to hardship and tragedy when the Civil War began. Terrifying new sounds of war traveled fast across the water, from Fort Fisher to Wrightsville Sound. Many Sound residents refugeed to inland cities. Some of those who had houses in town had unwanted guests as Union troops took control of the finer residences. Even boats at the Carolina Yacht Club were confiscated by the Yankees.

Sadness was compounded when Dr. Wright died on September 21, 1861. Already, the charmed existence he had known had begun to erode in the late 1850s. His wife, Mary Allan, was blinded and disfigured in an accident, in 1856, and symptoms somewhat consistent with severe rheumatoid arthritis compromised the doctor's health. Dr. Wright's own physician and pharmacist, Dr. William B. Giles, did what he could, but the prevalent local drugs of the day — camphor, paregoric, and laudanum, could do little to heal.[30]

Dr. Wright's death shook a great many Wilmingtonians despite many distractions, and grieved the soundfront community. "From my earliest childhood, I had learned to love the Doctor, and in my mind he has even been associated with all that is good and right. How I used to love to see him in the little pulpit at the Sound! How I loved to hear him reading the beautiful service of our church; for there was always so much fervor and so much warmth in his manner," wrote John Reston Giles, to Dr. Wright's widow, September 26, 1861. John Giles, who was stationed at Thunderbolt Battery at the time, would become yet another Civil War casualty, dying July 8, 1863.[31]

Other tragedies unfolded for the Soundfront residents. Two of Dr. Wright's sons died on the battlefield, including James Allan, the first little baby baptized at Mount Lebanon. Another son, Joshua Grainger Wright, was severely wounded. Many of the Wrights' close friends, including the Rev. Dr. Drane, died in the yellow fever epidemic of 1862. What was left of the family refugeed to Fayetteville. Their Wilmington town home was commandeered in 1865 by Union General Joseph R. Hawley, and St. James Church was violated by Northern troops and used as a hospital. When the war ended, the Burgwin-Wright House became a Confederate hospital and was filled with "starving, sick and rotten men."[32]

Following the Civil War, many Wright properties changed hands as the family struggled to adjust to dramatic financial losses. Dr. Wright's family was hit harder than most wealthy Southern clans because of his deep involvement in the Bank of Cape Fear, an institution rendered as worthless as a Confederate bill. After Mary Allan Wright's death, in 1866, the couple's eldest son, Dr. Adam Empie Wright, inherited the Burgwin-Wright House and Mount Lebanon. A graduate of the University of North Carolina and New York University of Medicine, Dr. Adam Wright was a surgeon. Despite his vocation, he found it necessary in 1869 to sell the family home at Third and Market, for $5000. By 1871, Adam Wright had established a pharmacy partnership with J. K. McIlhenny. They advertised medications "cheaper than any Drug House South of New York."

Meanwhile, St. James Church members, most of whom had strong Sound connections, continued to lead Mount Lebanon. In 1877, Clayton Giles was appointed lay reader and engaged the help of William B. Giles and Charles D. Myers to sustain services at the chapel. That same year, the building was insured for $1000. The premium was paid by funds raised from summer congregations, led by the Rev. Alfred A. Watson, rector of St. James, who was elected Bishop of the Diocese of East Carolina on December 13, 1883.

Dr. Adam Wright continued his private practice, seeing patients at his office, located at the foot of Mulberry (Grace) Street, until 1878. In 1879, after suffering for years from what he termed his "father's disease," Adam Wright died, at the age of 46. His two young sons, Adam, Jr., and Marion, inherited Mount Lebanon.[33]

Since the Civil War, the Sound house had proven to be convenient year-round lodging for several members of the family, including newlyweds Mr. and Mrs. Clayton Giles, and a busy place in summer. It must have been heart-breaking for the entire family when Mount Lebanon was sold in 1881. Adam and Marion Wright's guardian, Marion Potter, a relative of the boys' mother, Sarah Potter Wright, signed the deed to Margaret Schutte. Marion Potter also deeded the Mount Lebanon Chapel tract to St. James Church, a legality curiously omitted by a family full of attorneys. Members of the vast Wright family continued to frequent services at the chapel, thus keeping a tie to the land. The blow of losing the Sound house was softened emotionally by retaining a two-acre waterfront strip of land, the only portion of the southern Mount Lebanon tract that still remains in the hands of Judge Joshua Grainger Wright's descendants.

"This reserved tract," the deed reads, "part of the land being excepted from the conveyance for the purpose of preserving in the family of the late Dr. Thos. H. Wright and portion of the homestead which has been immemorially in that family and not with the intent of simply diminishing the size of the tract granted, it is distinctly agreed and consented between the parties of these present.....that descendants of the late Thomas H. Wright shall have the privilege of being the purchasers or lessees in preference to all other persons." Today, 201 years after Judge Wright purchased Mount Lebanon, Eleanor Wright Beane, his great-great granddaughter, owns the two-acre "Exception," along with the expansive William Augustus Wright tract, "Gabriel's Landing," on the north side of Airlie curve.[34]

William A. Wright, who owned the property "across the street" from Airlie Gardens, was the force behind the creation of the road, from 17th Street to Wrightsville Sound, in 1874. Earlier efforts by others had failed. A brother of Dr. Thomas Wright, William Wright's activities were nearly as diverse: attorney for various large businesses, including the Wilmington and Weldon Railroad; president of the Bank of Cape Fear; president of the Cape Fear Club and Commodore of the Carolina Yacht Club, from 1874 until 1878; a director of Oakdale Cemetery, who actually planted the original oaks, and a New Hanover County land baron. His real estate holdings exceeded but included what we know now as Carolina Heights, Carolina Place, the entire Delgado-Spofford Mill tract, and the four-story Hill-Wright-Wootten House that sat just south of St. James Church. He owned "Dove Cote," a charming cottage crafted by a carpenter named "Bird" that still stands, at 712 Market Street. Additionally, he held an interest in the Wright-Harriss-Bellamy House, on the southeast corner of Sixth and Market. He also possessed great swaths of what is now Wrightsville Avenue, and a quarry three miles north, near the Delgado site. The quarry yielded small rock, mixed with sharks' teeth and other petrified sea life, from which macadam roads were paved.[35]

On Wrightsville Sound, William Wright's neighbor to the south was, as always, his brother, Dr. Thomas Wright. His neighbors to the north were mostly relatives and good friends of the Wright family who purchased land from his father, Judge Wright, before 1811. They bought deep strips that ranged from 20 1/2 to 32 acres, tracts that are now the site of Edgewater, Gray Gables, the Weathers-McCarl House and many other properties on the west side of Airlie Road. Even so, the William A. Wright tract measured over 100 acres, although it had diminished to 38.7 acres when heirs of William A. Wright III sold it to Frank Beane, August 12, 1929.[36]

The Shell Road served Mr. Wright in a number of ways. His frequent trips to the Sound were made easier because of the much-improved thoroughfare, it increased the value of land he owned up and down Shell Road, and it made quite a bit of business for his rock quarry. Also, he sold a small tract at the intersection of 17th Street and Wrightsville Avenue, as a site for a toll booth. For years, the triangular plaza was carefully manicured by firemen, planted in azaleas and adorned with a stone birdbath and a statue of a boy going fishing. Mrs. Wright McGowan, wife of Airlie supervisor Francis Marion McGowan, kept the toll booth at Dock and 17th for twenty years. When completed, the turnpike was beautiful. Usually quiet, it made traveling a pleasure, with its natural oak arches and sun-bleached shells. It was especially picturesque at night. "A ride to the Sound over the turnpike is delightful these beautiful moonlit nights. Try it and see," swore one local reporter, in 1890.[37]

Shell roads were made in 1874 much as they were in 1930, when George Evans helped build additional paths at Airlie. "Hundreds of years ago, when Indians were down here, they ate clams and oysters and they would leave the shells," said Mr. Evans. "That stuff stayed out at the edge of the Sound - five or six feet deep in the ground. We used to go down there and dig that stuff out. It was called Indian Embankment. We would haul it up on the shore and then come back and spread it out on the road.

"I used to have to dig that stuff out of the Sound and it was hard work. The only way you could get it was at low tide. After the tide crept out, you had to go out and load it onto a boat, row in and roll it up from the wet shore on planks, about 12 feet long. There wasn't such a thing as wheelbarrows - we had Georgia buggies with iron wheels. We had to roll that stuff to the shore and dump it before the tide came back in. If we started digging one day and the tide

A fisherman poles a small boat in Bradley Creek, while a dressed up steam launch sits idle, about 1895. A Georgia buggy sits on the pier. (Lower Cape Fear Historical Society)

came and caught us, well, when we went out the next day, we'd have to pump the water out of that hole. At high tide, it would be four to six feet deep.

"Then we'd spread it out and there was a heavy big roller and horses would pull the steel roller over the shell roads to flatten them out," said Mr. Evans.

The oldest shell paths on the Airlie property were built before 1855 as narrow dirt roads. Meandering around the perimeter of Bradley Creek and the Sound, they were described as "a road or way of suitable width for the passage of ordinary vehicles." They were paved in shells in the 1870s, making passage easier for horses and horse drawn transportation, but have frustrated any workmen who have had to dig through them since. [38]

Wilmingtonians Henry and George Haar supervised construction of the 1874 shell road. According to historian Henry Bacon McKoy, prices on the road about 1915 were 25 cents for a buggy, 20 for horseback, 15 per cart, a dime for a bicycle and 50 cents for a horse and carriage. Those lucky enough to have four horses and a carriage paid a dollar. Once paid, the gatekeeper pulled a lever and a large wooden arm anchored at the toll booth was raised, allowing access.[39]

The road benefited the new owners of the Lebanon tract, now described as being located on the "southern line of Wilmington and Coast Turnpike." The Schuttes constructed an inn nearby. The small hotel, powered by a windmill, was known variously as Schutte's Grove, Oak Grove, Grove Park, and Sea Side Park Hotel. Italian harpers and Chinese lanterns lured locals in for Wednesday night seafood dinners, but times were tough during Reconstruction and the hotel did not thrive. The Schuttes sold it to James Chadbourn in 1882, and he deeded it to an establishment known as the Seaside Park Improvement Company. With that transaction, the property entered a new era, for Mr. Pembroke Jones was president of the firm. Ambitious, entertaining, robustly friendly, yet essentially elusive, Jones would become Wilmington's living legend. He inspired at least one song and, with his wife, caused the coining of the phrase "keeping up with the Joneses." He rose from being a motherless child with an absent father to creating a sturdy social network that included some of America's wealthiest and most powerful individuals.[40]

Sarah and Pembroke

Born December 15, 1858, the son of Lt. John Pembroke Jones and Jane Vance London, young Pembroke had solid parentage. His father, who hailed from Pembroke Farm, near Hampton, Virginia, was a graduate of William and Mary and the U. S. Naval Academy, where he ranked first in mathematics and proved his valor: his collegiate senior project was participation in the Siege of Buena Vista during the Mexican War. In 1849, he fought a famous duel with future poet James Barron Hope, another "scion of the first families of Virginia," over an unfortunate remark Hope made about Jones's brother, Tom. The two men stood at ten paces, shot one another, mumbled mutual concern as they lay wounded, recovered, and became fast friends and members of the same Tidewater Virginia Episcopal church. Pembroke Jones's mother, belonging to Wilmington's vast Bradley-Wright-London-Cowan family tree, was the daughter of Bank of Cape Fear president John London. Further complicating Wilmington's "cousinhood," John London's niece, Mary, daughter of his brother, Mauger London, would marry Captain Pembroke Jones's brother, Colonel Tom Jones, in 1864.

Little Pembroke was baptized in venerable St. James Church in the sight of God and clergy and innumerable relatives on January 30, 1859. But when he was only three months old, the baby's mother died and his father was already established in a career dependent upon travel. Already, for ten years before the baby's birth, Lt. Jones had worked as a civil engineer, surveying the east coast of North Carolina and Virginia. In 1851, he served on the coast and geodetic survey schooner *Gallatin*, under the command of Lieut. Commander John Newland Maffitt. The two men became devoted and lifelong friends as well as relatives by marriage: Captain Maffitt's daughter, Florie, married Jane London Jones's cousin, Joshua Grainger Wright, in 1865. Many years later, when Maffitt's third wife, Emma, published a biography of the captain, *The Life and Services of John Newland Maffitt*, Pembroke Jones, Jr., purchased a hundred copies, in honor of his father's friendship with Maffitt.[41]

John Pembroke Jones, father of Airlie owner Pembroke Jones (Hampton History Museum)

With his mother gone and his father often out on the open seas, little Pembroke needed fostering. One of his maternal aunts, Alice Heron London Dickinson, took her nephew in and cared for him as her own. Her husband, Platt Ketchum Dickinson, was a successful lumberman who is credited with the idea of establishing Wilmington's first railroad, the Wilmington and Weldon. Platt Dickinson had been married once, to Jane Vance, who died May 8, 1828, of tuberculosis. Sixteen years later, on November 27, 1845, he married Alice London, twenty years his junior. Though Dickinson had children by a previous marriage, Alice had none of her own. The guardianship became official when Captain Pembroke Jones gave Platt Dickinson power of attorney to handle business matters for his young son.[42]

While Pembroke Jones was still a pampered toddler, his father was assigned to duty on the *Congress,* off the coast of Africa. Eventually he contracted African fever and was sent to New Orleans to convalesce. By the time he reached the States, Louisiana had seceded from the Union. When Jones landed, he was arrested as a traitor because he was wearing blue. He telegrammed his resignation from the U. S. Navy and began serving in the Confederate States Navy.

By June 1861, Captain Jones was stationed at Pig Point Battery at the mouth of the Nansemond River, defending Portsmouth, Virginia, and the Navy Yard. "Tell Mr. London," he wrote to his sister, Emilie London, of Wilmington, "I think if they hurry in getting guns at all the inlets of N. C. that his State is safe for a long time. Tell him also that I have a Battery of 10 guns and if the enemy attempts to approach Portsmouth and Navy Yard by Nansemond River we will have a big fight."[43]

Captain Jones was an officer on the *Merrimac* during the second battle with the *Monitor*. He also commanded the *Georgia* and, in 1864, the ironclad blockade running sloop, *Raleigh*, built in Wilmington, by J. L. Cassidey and Sons. This vessel, laid out and launched at the foot of Church Street, had four guns, weighed 600 tons and cost about $50,000. The *Raleigh* attacked and broke through the Cape Fear blockade, but was wrecked accidentally in 1864, in the Cape Fear River. One observer stated that the remains of the *Raleigh*, off Fort Fisher, had the appearance of a monstrous turtle, stranded and forlorn.

In 1864, Captain Jones was married a second time, to Mary Willis, of Savannah. They had a son who took his maternal grandfather's entire name: Edward Jones Willis. As the war's resolution became apparent to Captain Jones, he warned those in Wilmington. "This second letter of Mr. Pembroke Jones begins to show that all is not gold that glitters," wrote Alice deRosset, in January 1865, "and the tigers' claws peep out of the velvet fur."[44]

After the war, the Joneses moved to Airlie Farm, in Fauquier County, Virginia, but did not stay there long. Capt. Jones continued his engineering pursuits and charted new territory when he surveyed the Rio de la Plata for the Argentine Republic. He also charted Argentinean railway paths and established military defenses before moving to Europe for the sake of his health. At Jones's death in Pasadena, California, May 25, 1910, he was the oldest graduate of the U. S. Naval Academy. He left a third wife, Georgia Newton, of Norfolk, Va.

"Captain Jones was a man of most charming personality," wrote one of his peers, "and his wealth of experience and intercourse through the years of service in all parts of the world and association with master minds and the refined society of many countries made him a most interesting companion for young and old. His shipmates and classmates spoke of his ability, his charm of character and the poetic beauty of his imagination."[45]

A World War I housing community for shipbuilders, in Hampton, Virginia, was named Hilton Village, in honor of the Joneses' original home there.

Though Pembroke Jones's father was an accomplished man, he was almost entirely absent from his eldest child's life. Platt Dickinson, his foster father, was a strong force, accomplished in business and given to good deeds. In addition to contributing the bell and tower clock to St. James Church, in 1840, he gave so much general financial support that he was rewarded with a free lot in the church cemetery. Surely Mr. Dickinson provided a good role model for young Pembroke, but he died May 12, 1867, when the boy was only eight years old. Alice Dickinson continued to live in the big Dickinson house, bounded by Front and Chestnut streets and their respective alleys: Vance and Dickinson. With money inherited from her father and husband, she provided a good life for her beloved nephew. When he was at school, she busied herself with church activities and her other favorite "community service": the

Mount Vernon Association. She served as vice-regent of the organization dedicated originally to the purchase of George Washington's home. She collected at least enough money for the cause to receive national attention.

It would seem a remote cause except that Alice grew up hearing tales of Washington from her father, who in turn heard them from Alexander Hamilton, whose acquaintance he made September 21 and 22, 1800, when the two men were both guests at Butler's Tavern, in New Haven, Connecticut. "General Hamilton told us," said John London, "that General Washington, notwithstanding his perfect regularity and love of decorum, could bear to drink more wine than most people. He loved to make a procrastinated dinner...made it a rule to drink a glass of wine with every one at the table and yet always drank three or four glasses of wine after dinner, according to his company....and every night took a pint of cream and toasted crust for supper."[46]

The Platt Dickinson House, at 200 North Front Street (Cape Fear Museum)

Pembroke grew up on the northeast corner of Front and Chestnut streets and received his local education at Cape Fear Academy. His first bit of local publicity came in 1873, when he was fourteen. There were no livestock restrictions in downtown Wilmington at that time. Possibly when Pembroke Jones exhibited a pair of chickens and a black mare named Alice at the fifth annual fair of the Cape Fear Agricultural Association, he plucked the livestock from his own backyard. The next time Jones made news, in 1878, was in tandem with his future close friend and business partner, Norwood Giles.

Giles, named for his mother's sister's husband, Dr. John W. Norwood, was a Civil War veteran. When only fifteen, he had joined North Carolina Troop, Company E, Tenth Regiment. Listing "Trenches" as his return address, young Norwood wrote his father of his dietary changes since leaving the abundant seafood and fresh vegetables of the Sound: "I get plenty to eat - wheat bread all the time and fresh beef occasionally. We can buy a cow's head (without tongue) for two or three dollars and two good sized pumpkins for one, but have to bring them five miles on our shoulders. "

Norwood survived battles and skirmishes against what he called the "Lilliputian Cavalry" and returned home to Edge Hill, on the Sound. He established a rice milling business and quickly became known as an excellent yachtsman. In 1875, a benchmark occurred in local boating history. The steamship *Benefactor* arrived at Wilmington with a delivery for Norwood Giles: the yacht *Ripple*. The *Ripple*, a legendary skiff, became famous for winning many regattas and for the small parties held aboard her.

On April 20, 1878, Norwood Giles took on a new racing partner: 19-year-old Pembroke Jones crewed with him on the rowing barge *White Swan*. The vessel was 28 feet long and carried 12-foot oars. The two men, both stiff competitors, raced against and with each other for the next twenty years. In 1884, the same year Pembroke Jones won a regatta in *Rosa*, he was named commodore of the Carolina Yacht Club and served until 1886. "Our Commodore is young and handsome," wrote Norwood Giles. Indeed he was. Well-dressed, slender, quick-moving, with resolute visage, Jones cut an elegant and powerful figure.

Though he had many boats, Pembroke Jones's principal local craft became the *Idler*. He also raced the *Vixen*, a yacht he sold eventually to Herbert Latimer. Jones and railroad executive Henry Walters shared ownership of the *Glide* and *Pegotty*. In fact, the two men probably became close friends through yachting. Walters visited Wilmington with increasing frequency, beginning about 1878. By 1892, he owned a house situated on a double lot, three lots south the Carolina Yacht Club. Jones and Walters kept other yachts at Narragansett and in New York, where he and Henry Walters were members of the New York Yacht Club.[47]

Many of the Sound boats also raced and cruised on the Cape Fear. Airlie neighbor Edward S. Latimer raced the *Vixen*, May 30, 1895, from the foot of Market Street south to a red buoy at the Dram Tree four miles away, and back again. The *Vixen* won the race in one hour, 50 minutes. On August 9, 1895, Capt. H. G. Latimer's Wrightsville yacht *Pastime* carried a party of Wilmingtonians to Point Caswell, 36 miles up the Cape Fear and Black rivers. "She not only walked the waters like a thing of life, but made a fine record for speed, making the trip back in less than 3 hours."[48]

Norwood Giles and Pembroke Jones created their own business in 1879: Carolina Rice Mills. In 1880, they erected a four-story brick office building at the foot of Chestnut Street, just west of the James Dawson House, now the site of the First Union Bank Building. Daily, Carolina Rice Mills processed 75 to 100 barrels of rough rice into clean grains. In the words of an 1884 publication, the rice at Carolina Rice Mills "first passed through a set of stone, where it is ground, then to pestles, eighteen in number, thence it passes through the brushes for polishing.... and necessary fans and screens."

After only five years in operation, Jones and Giles, described as "in the prime of vigorous manhood," had established branches in New York, Cincinnati, London, Charlotte, Norfolk, Richmond, Lynchburg and Kansas City. Norwood Giles moved to New York to manage milling interests, but was also caught up in the business of railroads through another friend, General William MacRae of Wilmington and Augusta. After Giles died in New York, December 11, 1899, the building at 7 Chestnut Street was sold. On January 25, 1922, fire destroyed the building. By that time, it housed Pearsall and Company, owned by Airlie Road resident Horace Pearsall, and was a storage space for the household furnishings of Herbert Latimer, next-door neighbor to Airlie Gardens. Ironically, by that time, Herbert Latimer's residence, Lebanon, was a storage place for Mrs. Henry Walters.[49]

Sarah Green and Pembroke Jones were married soon after the rice mill became a success, on Thanksgiving Day, November 27, 1884. The bride's family lived at Tokay, a 469-acre scuppernong vineyard, located three miles north of Fayetteville in the Cape Fear Valley. The Greens were descendants of Sir John Hawkins, a cousin of Sir Francis Drake and a British hero in the defeat of the Spanish Armada, in 1588. Sarah's father, Colonel Wharton J. Green, purchased Tokay in 1879, and by the mid-1880s it was known as the largest vineyard east of the Rockies. Henry Walters, who became general manager of the Wilmington and Weldon Railroad, in 1884, gave Tokay his Midas touch when he engineered the construction of the "Fayetteville Cut-off," a million-dollar extension of the line that was as beneficial to Col. Green's vineyard business as oxygen to a bonfire. Today, like Pembroke Park, Tokay has been subdivided. The new developments include neighborhoods called Tokay and Sadie Heights.[50]

Col. Green, himself the son of General Thomas Jefferson Green, had roots at Esmeralda, a 900-acre plantation in Warren County. General Thomas J. Green, described interestingly as noble, generous, impulsive, and fiery, was educated at the University of North Carolina and the United States Military Academy. A leader during the Texas Revolution, he helped establish the boundaries between the U. S. and Mexico and was one of the first advocates of a cross-country railroad. He married Sarah Angeline Wharton, daughter of U. S. Senator Jesse Wharton, of Nashville, Tennessee. Before the Civil War, he moved back to North Carolina where he bred racehorses and entertained lavishly. On May 4, 1858, Col. Green's son, Wharton, married his step-sister, Esther Sargent Ellery, a prominent Bostonian. Their wedding took place at Montmorenci, another Warren County plantation. The Greens' honeymoon consisted of a fourteen-month tour of Europe and Egypt, where they cruised the Nile. Soon after they returned to Boston, Sarah was born July 19, 1859. When she was a month old, the Greens moved back to Esmeralda.

The Civil War years brought change and heartache to the family. General Green died in 1863, while his son, Wharton, was a prisoner of war at Johnson's Island, along with family friend Col. Thomas Kenan. Little Sarah continued to live at Esmeralda during and after the war. Eventually the Green family grew to be five. Though the youngest daughter died at an early age, three survived: Sarah Wharton, Caroline (Carrie) Adeline and Mable Ellery.[51]

After the war, Col. Green taught at Georgetown, a situation that poses an interesting question. Did Henry Walters, who was a member of the Class of 1869, meet there the young girl who would become his future wife, Sarah Green? If so, it would be a half century before he married her, before he married anyone. After Georgetown, he attended Harvard's Lawrence Scientific School, where he graduated, in 1873.

The Wharton Greens were still living at Esmeralda, in 1873, when Sarah left for school. She attended Notre Dame of Maryland Collegiate Institute for Young Ladies, known now as The Notre Dame College of Maryland, in Baltimore County, for the next four years. There she studied everything from German to elocution, penmanship to back-stitching, and physics to Christian doctrine. She expressed interest in becoming a Roman Catholic but apparently never converted.[52]

Among other honors, Sarah Green graduated as class valedictorian, June 28, 1877. Her speech actually was a lengthy poem she wrote entitled, "Ships that go out to sea." The little girl who would spend so much of her adult life both on and within sight of water wrote of vessels and people and of young women who graduate and sail off in different directions.

"I stood one day, upon a pier,
And watched the stately vessels near
As on the waters free from strife
They seemed to rock like things of life
For us, Oh let your prayer then be
The ships that this year go to sea."[53]

It's notable that Sarah Green and Henry Walters had Catholic school graduation speeches in common. Walters delivered his, in 1869, at Georgetown. The only speech he is known to have made, it was entitled, "A Plea for Manhood." Sarah's former classmates elected her honorary president of the college's alumni association, 1896-97.

In 1879, the Greens moved from Esmeralda to Tokay. By then, Sarah, twenty years old, was the unassuming version of Scarlett O'Hara at the Twin Oaks picnic, whether at Tokay or Wilmington, White Sulphur Springs, in West Virginia, or Martha's Vineyard. In 1882, when Col. Green was elected Third District Representative to the 48th U. S.

Congress, he took his whole family with him to Washington. However it was Sarah who became the "reigning belle at the Federal Capital." Filling in for her mother who was ill, Sarah not only captivated Washington society with her hospitality, she in turn was snared by the pleasure of entertaining. The thrill she felt when she played hostess to hundreds of happy guests would need to be realized at short intervals throughout her lifetime. Her hostess duties increased when Mrs. Green died, in June 1883.[54]

In 1884, when Sarah Wharton Green, of Fayetteville, married Pembroke Jones, of Wilmington, it was eastern North Carolina's answer to a royal wedding. The bride's father issued invitations to the 8:00 p.m. service at St. John's Church. Decorations included a marriage bell made of camellias, carnations and roses, arches made of smilax, and a floral horseshoe. Though Capt. Pembroke Jones, father of the groom, attended, Wilmington native Charles Bruce Wright, a grandson of Judge Joshua G. Wright, served as best man. Charles Wright would soon marry Ella Holt, daughter of N. C. Governor Thomas Holt, of Haw River Mill fame. After the service, the bride's father provided "supper" for 1000 at Tokay. The approach to the plantation was lit by colorful lanterns and the ten connecting rooms of the house were decorated to represent the palace of an Eastern potentate. "The rarest delicacies from many lands and the costliest wines were served in an abandon of profusion."

Guests included Sam Strange, Ben R. Huske, Fred Kidder, Wright Meares, P. L. Bridgers, B. G. Empie, and the ministers who conducted the service, John Huske and Robert Strange. Gifts poured in as well from guests, among them Green, Murchison, Sprunt, Wright, Strange, Emerson, Empie, McKoy, Smallbones, Haywood, Daniels, Davis, Orrell, Willis, Cronly, McRary and Anderson families. Most of the presents were sterling flatware, but Derby vases, cut glass pitchers, and a money box were also part of the glittering treasures. Fred Kidder gave them a painting and Bennehan Cameron of Durham County brought 12 silver spoons and a silver-and-gold ice cream knife. Someone who wished to be "anonymous" gave them a hand-painted scroll, a tempting hint that Col. Green's friend, Henry Walters, was on the guest list.

The wedding reception went on for hours as guests celebrated with toast after toast. Guests also offered a prayer of some amusement that by the time death parted the couple, they could still agree that Thanksgiving was an appropriate day for their anniversary. At 3:00 a.m., the bride and groom boarded a train for New York where they honeymooned briefly before returning to Washington, where Sarah continued her duties as "lady of her father's household" during the Congressional session. For the next few years, Sarah and Pembroke lived in Washington a portion of every year.[55]

In the spring of 1885, Pembroke Jones offered "for rent the summer resort of Sea Side Park, including the hotel." On May 13, 1884, before she married Pembroke Jones, "Sarah W. Green, of Cumberland County, N. C." purchased the 52-acre Seaside Park Improvement Company on Wrightsville Sound, for $5,000. After their marriage, it was usually identified as the groom's property but remained in Sarah's name.

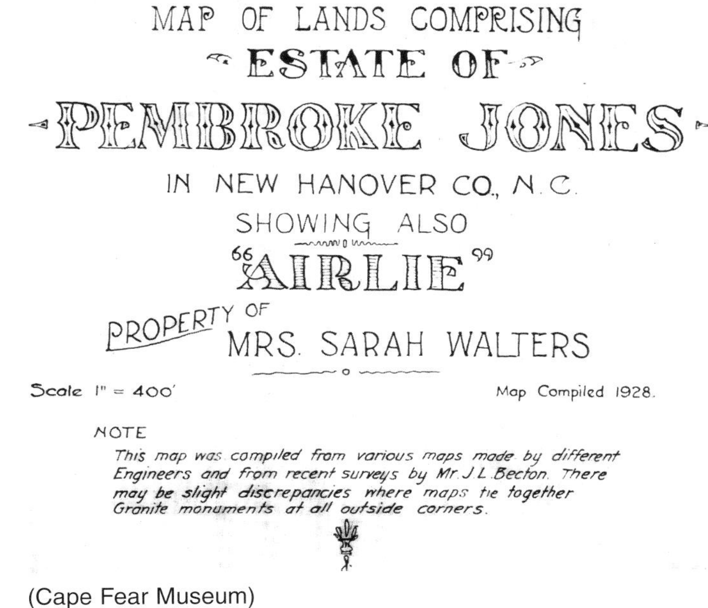

(Cape Fear Museum)

On September 22, 1885, just ten months after her wedding, Sarah Jones bought another prominent New Hanover County property: 400 South Front Street, known today as the Governor Dudley Mansion. She paid $11,000 for the imposing 60-year-old residence. Though only 26, she found herself owning two premier New Hanover County properties, a rare thing for a young woman in those days. The house on South Front Street, already famous as the site of organizational meetings of the Wilmington and Weldon Railroad, in the 1830s, and a reception for Daniel Webster, in 1847, and James Cardinal Gibbons, in 1885, was well-suited for the hospitable couple. The location was even more attractive because their friends, the William Rand Kenans, lived just around the corner, at 110 Nun Street.[56]

On April 5, 1886, a portion of Sea Side Park was offered for sale. It didn't wait long for a buyer: 21 days later, Seaside Park Improvement Company divided the parcel and transferred a portion of Sarah Jones's property to Herbert R. Latimer. The Joneses' and Latimers' sociable paths crossed in downtown Wilmington as well as on the Sound, where Latimers already owned one summer home, next to Edge Hill. A marble post just off Airlie Road, "Seaside Fork," marked the new Latimer residence and that of the Joneses. One side read "HRL"; the other, "PJ." [57]

Herbert Latimer's tract, where he already resided as a tenant, included the Mount Lebanon house that he called simply Lebanon. Mr. Latimer had wed Frances Fielding Lewis Empie, Dr. Thomas Henry Wright's grandniece, on June 11, 1884. Their honeymoon, "a protracted tour of Europe," went on until December. Unfortunately, after returning to Wilmington, Herbert Latimer had little time to enjoy married life or Lebanon. He died July 11, 1887, of tuberculosis, a disease that rendered him an invalid even before he purchased the summer tract.

Herbert and Empie Latimer (Lower Cape Fear Historical Society)

Herbert Latimer's widow and two sons, Herbert Russell Latimer, Jr., and Empie Latimer, continued to vacation on the Sound. Their cousins, the Zebulon and Edward Latimers, lived nearby, on the south side of the creek. Herbert, Jr., was born on Wrightsville Sound, August 16, 1885, and baptized at Mount Lebanon Chapel. He attended a private school in Heidelberg, Germany, before enrolling in Princeton. After graduation, in 1908, he earned a degree in mine engineering from Columbia, in 1912. He designed mine operations in Utah and Michigan before enlisting in the British Army in 1916. For meritorious service in Ypres, Amiens and many of the final engagements of the war, he was awarded the British Military Cross.

Empie Latimer, born December 5, 1886, followed the same school and career path as his brother. In 1914, they even bet in tandem on a long shot at the English Derby. The "rank outsider" won, creating a new windfall for the privileged young men. However, they parted dramatically, late in 1915, when Empie entered the American Ambulance

Service in France. He witnessed the battle of the Somme and the fighting around Verdun before returning, after ten months of service. He returned home for Christmas in 1916, but he and brother Herbert were both at war by August 1917. The older brother sailed to England, while Empie boarded a French liner for Le Havre where he enlisted in the American Field Service. Empie saw combat in 1918 and was burned by mustard gas. "After an explosion of ammunition at his battery, he crawled through the flames under shell fire in order to separate the powder that remained and save the lives of men and materials at the battery," wrote his brother, Herbert. By the war's end, he had been wounded twice and received three American citations, as well as the Croix de Guerre with Palm by the French government. [58]

Both brothers returned to Wilmington where they lived the rest of their lives as retired Southern gentlemen. By 1920 their mother, who had remarried and was now Fannie Empie Latimer Poisson, had deeded Mount Lebanon to Empie. Herbert was compensated. Empie took great pleasure in repairing and restoring the "old place," but soon after he finished redoing the house, Mrs. Walters made him an offer he couldn't refuse. From the 1920s until her estate was settled, after 1941, Sarah Walters and her heirs leased Lebanon.

"At one time, said George Evans, "the Latimers weren't living there and Mrs. Walters used the place. She would stack a lot of furniture there. When things would get too crowded at the big house, she'd say, 'Take this over there.'"

"Mrs. Walters also kept a speed boat at the Latimers'. George Kidder gave it to her. She kept it at a little boat house down there."[59]

In 1947, the *Princeton Alumni Weekly* reported that they "found Herbert and Empie Latimer in Wilmington, N. C., looking young and handsome. Time has dealt gently with them. During the winter they live with their aunt in the antebellum home in Wilmington (126 South Third Street) and during the pleasant months they stay at their country place on salt water. They speak of it as the Sound."[60]

Empie Latimer died January 3, 1948, at the age of 61. In 1963, Herbert Latimer deeded his uncle's home at 126 South Third Street to the Lower Cape Fear Historical Society. Despite his interest in local history, he burned hundreds of Latimer family letters shortly before his death, November 5, 1966.

Fannie Empie Latimer (Lower Cape Fear Historical Society)

Eventually the abandoned Wright-Latimer Sound house became bait for adventurous teenagers. Many Wilmingtonians who were adolescents in the 1960s and 70s poked their way through the elevated floorboards to explore the creaking old residence, a structure full of such ancient memories that its original owners had been long forgotten. The house, located in what is now known as Bradley Creek Point, was razed in the 1970s. The Rebecca Laymon residence now occupies the spot. Author Anne Russell, Mrs. Laymon's next-door neighbor, is descended from Susan Bradley Wright's brother, Richard Bradley, Jr. (1769-1834). West of the Mount Lebanon House, the Joneses continued to create their own history. In 1887, following a meeting of a "party of gentlemen," the Joneses' residence at Airlie caught fire. The house was a total loss, but the Joneses rebuilt promptly.

Pembroke Jones was active in Wilmington's social clubs, retaining memberships in the Carolina Yacht Club, L'Arioso German Club, the Cape Fear Club, and Cape Fear Country Club. On April 17, 1891, Jones became a member of a much smaller group, the Oak Point Club. Along with Henry Walters, Judge Addison Ricaud and John Daniel, they drew a charter entirely predictive of what was to come: "The proposed business of said corporation is the conducting of a pleasure club for social and literary purposes, and the mutual benefit and recreation of its members and also the establishment and maintenance of fishing and hunting grounds, and the providing of other innocent and lawful amusements for its members."[61]

"The Oak Point club," according to the charter, also "proposes to purchase for said purposes real estate situated in New Hanover county, on the east side of Lee's or Bradley's creek, where it empties into the sound near the Atlantic Ocean."

Another change came to Airlie when the Wilmington Sea-Coast Railroad Company made the Sound a stop rather than a destination. Traffic increased greatly because for the first time, tourists and landowners could visit the Hammocks, now known as Harbor Island, by train. William Latimer and James Chadbourn, principals of the enterprise, presided at ceremonies on June 16, 1888, to drive the "Silver Spike," marking the completion of the "bands of steel, reaching from the city to the sea." Invited guests enjoyed a private ride in canary-colored cars from the streetcar stop at Front and Princess to the island.

"Those of you who can recall the ever generous and openhearted hospitality offered to visitors at the Sound will rejoice. Its healthful pleasures and innocent recreations can now be enjoyed by so much larger a number," said William Latimer. "Who a few short years ago, would have believed that the shunned and despised Hammocks, the resort of the solitary heron, and the breeding place of pestiferous insects, could be made to become so charming a place as it is now seen to be?"[62]

The train added a new dimension to church life. By the 1890s, services were held occasionally at the Hammocks. The Rev. Robert Strange led worship at Lebanon Chapel before riding the train to preside at the Island Beach Hotel. By 1895, he was conducting dual Sunday morning services, at Lebanon Chapel and Brown's Pavilion, a building that was replaced by the Seashore Hotel, on Wrightsville Beach.[63]

A two-wheel bicycle craze hit Wilmington in the 1890s, and one of the favorite cycling tracks was the Wilmington and Coast Turnpike. Henry Gould Latimer was the first person known to cycle at the Sound. He bought an English tricycle in Europe, in 1884. "A day or two since he made the run to Wrightsville Sound in forty minutes. ...That is to say, it (the 3-wheeled bicycle) reduces to the owner bills for advice, pain-killer and medical attention."

By 1897, Wrightsville Sound had become at least a seasonal home to many. Residents included G. W. Westbrook, W. G. Elliott, William A. Wright Jr., Hettie James, James Jackson, DuBrutz Cutlar, Mrs. T. H. Pritchard, Owen Fennell, L. L. Pritchard, Mrs. William Larkins, Clayton Giles, Col. J. W. Atkinson, Mrs. H. G. Daniel, L. A. Blue, W. H. Stokeley, George Harriss, J. F. Gause, William Blanks, William Latimer, Mrs. Fannie Poisson, Captain C.

S. Ellis, Oscar Pearsall, Marsden Bellamy, James H. Chadbourn, Jr., A. J. Flanner, the Ashley Gilbert estate, five cottages owned by M. J. Cronly, the Atlantic View Hotel and John Pembroke Jones, Jr.[64]

Cortachy Castle, Scotland

By 1897, Pembroke Jones had renamed his wife's soundfront property "Airlie," after his ancestral Scottish home. The earls of Airlie have occupied Cortachy Castle, in Angus, since 1625. The castle is situated on the banks of the South Esk, surrounded by woods and sheltered by the lower reaches of the Grampians. It stands at the entrance of Glen of Prosen, Clova, Doll and Moy. Pembroke Jones's father, Confederate Captain John Pembroke Jones, also named his home in northern Virginia "Airlie." Both estates featured lakes populated with swans.[65]

Pembroke Jones proved to be a good neighbor to Lebanon Chapel. He succeeded Clayton Giles, J. W. Atkinson and William A. Wright as supervisor for the building, but went a step further by financing all necessary maintenance. He considered the entire Mount Lebanon tract family land, since he was related to the Wrights through common descent from Elizabeth and Richard Bradley. He was fond of the little chapel and served as its patron and "custodian" off and on from 1883 until his death in 1919. Following Jones's death, W. B. Campbell supervised Lebanon's maintenance for several years.

No matter what good was wrought, the sale and renaming of part of the Wrights' Mount Lebanon tract and the acquisition of some additional Bradley acreage didn't set well with all the relatives. F. Ancrum Lord, a Bradley relation, wrote, in a letter partially inscribed in the margins of an 1891 Alexander Sprunt and Son daily cotton report: "Dear Pem, I have just heard that ugly remarks have been made of you and your wife by some of the younger portion of the Bradley family...There was, of course, a great deal of regret when the old place was sold."

Though the Bradley criticism would go on for at least a decade, Pembroke Jones was not moved by it. "I do not care what they say, or feel. Ask the younger members of the Bradley family to let me attend to my own affairs." Mr. Jones wrote on stationery imprinted simply, "Airlie, Wrightsville Sound, N. C."[66]

Sarah and Pembroke Jones celebrated their wooden, or fifth anniversary, November 27, 1889, with a party at 400 South Front Street. While telegrams were read from well-wishers as far away as New York, 250 of their closest friends enjoyed a lavish buffet. Six close friends of Sarah Jones assisted her: Carrie Strange, Janie Northrop, Callie Reid French, Jessie Kenan, Rosabelle Engelhard and Mrs. C. W. Kennedy. Italian harpists provided dance music and solo vocalists entertained the crowd. A local newspaper reporter called it a "happy event."[67]

However the following year was a sad one for them: Their eldest child, Alice Dickinson Jones, died February 7, at age four. She was survived by her two-year-old sibling, Sadie Green Jones, born April 13, 1887. On October 27, 1891, the couple's last child was born, a boy named for his father.

Never idle on the home improvement front, the Joneses made alterations inside their home and changed the exterior by adding a flamboyant porte cochere. Afternoon teas and evening soirees brought elegant guests and fancy carriages to the Joneses' handsome portal. They had a primitive cooling system that required large blocks of ice, delivered daily by "Uncle" Peter Hill. The house required a large staff of servants, many of whom would stay with them throughout Mrs. Jones's life.

Sadie Green Jones was born in an upstairs room at 400 South Front Street, in 1887. (Lower Cape Fear Historical Society)

The Enigmatic Mr. Walters

Henry Walters, always camera wary, sits at his desk in the Interstate Commerce Building. The Wilmington Railroad Museum houses a rare formal portrait of Mr. Walters. (Brown Brothers)

After the Joneses moved to 400 South Front Street, they acquired a new house guest, Henry Walters. Like his father, William Walters, he was a power in the railroad world. In 1884, Atlantic Coast Line directors named him general manager, but in 1902, he would add the titles Vice-President and Chairman of the Board, positions he would keep until 1931. Not only would he prove to be one of the nation's most proficient executives, smoothly merging 32 separate railroads into one, but he was also a world renowned art collector. His wealth and exquisite taste pervaded the Joneses' world, but his egoless ways make it impossible to ascertain where his influence and funding ended and Pembroke Jones's checkbook and flamboyance began. Quiet and studious, Walters was unlike Jones, who put little stock in solitary, reflective moments. The two men were like alternating zebra stripes.

Mr. Walters, though warm to friends and pleasant to servants, disliked being photographed and destroyed what he could of his own paper trail. He was reserved by nature, and his desire for privacy increased when he discovered his likeness in Horace Maclew, a character in Edith Wharton's 1924 novel, *The Mother's Recompense*. The *Wall Street Journal* summarized Walters's reticence: "He has succeeded so completely in effacing his personality and his acts, that he is not even a mystery. He is unknown."[68]

Walters, a Baltimore native, acquired his love of art during the Civil War when he and his family "refugeed" in Paris. His father, William Walters, having made money in the liquor business, began shopping for art, usually accompanied by his wife, Ellen. Sadly Ellen died of pneumonia while they were in Paris, but William Walters continued his artistic pursuits. Henry, a teenager, and his sister, Jennie, spent their days in Parisian schools, then came home to another kind of education in fine paintings, sculpture, tapestries and furnishings. Watching his father create an art collection lit inside the young man a fire that never went out, and created a bond between William and Henry Walters.

As an adult, Henry would become one of the nation's most important CEOs, but he continued to follow the trail of acquirable fine art, buying pieces that would be displayed in the art gallery in Baltimore, in the many homes he and the Joneses owned, for select friends, his family, and organizations like Wilmington's Cape Fear Club. Walters, who acquired 1700 items from Italy, known as the Massarenti Collection, in 1902, contributed several of the paintings to the Wilmington club, located on the southeast corner of Second and Chestnut streets. The Cape Fear Club, in turn, named its handsome library the Walters Reading Room.[69]

Though Walters and the Joneses had been acquainted for years, a Wilmington tradition probably contains some truth as to how they came to live together, about 1884. Henry Walters's yacht suffered mechanical trouble on an ocean cruise, near Cape Fear, and he was forced to pull into the nearest port. While Broadfoot Iron Works serviced the vessel, Walters stayed at the Orton, a hotel for which he probably orchestrated the 1880s redecoration. When Sarah Jones learned that he was in town, she sent an invitation by servant and invited him for a social visit. Though suffering from a brief illness, Walters attended. Pembroke Jones invited him to stay while he recuperated. Henry Walters recovered, but he never really left. Indeed, the three of them got along famously.[70]

According to William R. Johnston, Curator of the Walters Art Gallery in Baltimore, Mr. Walters's "interests were encyclopedic, ranging from third millennium cylinder seals to the 20th century art of Faberge." The Walters Art Gallery, which opened in 1934, was created from the private collection of Henry Walters and his father, William Walters.[71]

Henry Walters was good to his friends. Many of the Joneses' friends and relatives obtained positions of honor with the Atlantic Coast Line, including George Blow Elliott who became attorney and titular president of the railroad. Mr. Elliott was married to Mable Ellery Green Elliott, Sarah Jones's sister. Pembroke Jones served as a director and had a small town on the A. C. L. line named for him: Pembroke, N. C.[72]

In 1895, history almost repeated itself when the Governor Dudley caught fire. Though the house was not destroyed, the Joneses decided to move to their "shack," a rapidly enlarging retreat on the site of the old inn. Sarah and Pembroke Jones sold 400 South Front Street to a friend of his father's, James Sprunt, on February 28, 1895. Though Sarah purchased it for $11,000, the fire took its toll. Proceeds of the Sprunt sale were only $7000. Sprunt, a wealthy philanthropic cotton exporter, knew Pembroke Jones, Sr., from his Civil War days as a purser aboard a blockade runner. Both Sprunt and Pembroke Jones, Jr. were fond of yachting at Narragansett Bay, R. I. James Sprunt, along with his in-laws, the Murchisons, owned dwellings in a gracious compound of homes there.[73]

Sarah Jones with Pembroke III. Courtesy of Christine Leahy. (College of Notre Dame of Maryland Archives, Baltimore)

In 1896, even the privileged crowd at Narragansett must have been agog over Henry Walters's new purchase, an ocean-going, 224-foot long yacht that could carry a crew of up to 32 men and keep an average speed of 12 knots. It was built, in 1889, for M. Max LeBaudi, of Paris, who christened it *Semiramis*. Mr. LeBaudi soon sold it to Col. A. J. Drexel, of Philadelphia, who renamed it *Margarita*. Then Walters changed the name again. The *Narada*, the Indian word for Mercury, was already famous just months after Walters purchased it. "Mr. Walters arrived here yesterday morning," reported the *Norfolk Pilot*, "with a party of friends, consisting of Mr. Pembroke Jones and family; Mr. Fred Kidder and three charming ladies, all from North Carolina, who boarded the yacht for a summer cruise. (The *Narada*) is attracting considerable attention in the harbor."[74]

Walters and Pembroke Jones joined the New York Yacht Club, where Pembroke was the center of attention, a situation Mr. Walters always enjoyed. The New York *Sun* carried the following item, June 21, 1896. "Pembroke Jones, the owner of the 30-footer, *Carolina*, is quite a wag in his way, and in Tuesday's race, after calling for a drink and a sandwich, amused his guests by ordering the meal pennant hoisted on the grounds that he wished the crew to live up to yachting regulations on his boat or discipline could never be preserved."

Jones's humor and Sarah's unassuming charm went far to make friends. Elizabeth Drexel Lehr said Pembroke Jones was "a very merry man, getting the utmost flavor out of life, liking others to enjoy it, too." There was "no restraint at his parties."

Sarah Walters was not one to "put on airs." Her warmth, candor, and quick humor were disarming, and her entertainment budget, reported to be $300,000 a year, didn't impede the Joneses' social ascendancy. Henry Walters helped also. His money, connections, taste and the *Narada* lubricated their rise in social ranks. In fact, the *Narada* was such a part of their lives that the Joneses' young daughter, Sadie, when asked how one traveled to Europe, replied simply, "On Uncle Harry's yacht."[75]

The *Narada*, photographed by Charles Edwin Bolles. (Reprinted from: *William and Henry Walters: The Reticent Collectors*, by William R. Johnston. Mystic Seaport, Rosenfeld Collection, Mystic, Connecticut.)

The crew of the *Narada*. (Reprinted from: *William and Henry Walters: The Reticent Collectors*, by William R. Johnston. Mary Kane Hendrikson, New London, Connecticut.)

AIRLIE GARDENS

One of the most exquisite landmarks on the Sound is most surely the "Airlie Gardens" owned by the late Mr. & Mrs. Pembroke Jones and later Mr. & Mrs. Harry Walters.

The Gardens were made up of white wisteria, azaleas, roses, lilies, and other in season flowers under branches laden with spanish moss. The gardens were tended by a Mr. Topel from Germany and supervised by the late Mr. W. C. "Bud" Taylor.

This mansion was kept up by a large number of people, mostly from a small community of Black families along the road now called Airlie Road. They, along with others worked for the Jones and Walters holding different positions in this paradise, both on the grounds and in house.

Front Row: Eugene Hurst, Sr.
Back Row: L-R, Evelena Bernard, Maria Mandy, Jessie, Bertha DeBurnier, Margaret Mack, George Evans.

Front Row, L to R: Beulah Franks, Mable Mack, Mary Mack, Mary Anna Smith, Evelena Bernard.
Back Row: Margaret Mack, Millie Mack.

The lifestyle of the Jones and Walters was that of spectacular entertainment and anthropology.

Josephine Steadman

Preston Mack

Thomas A. Tartt

Charlie Whitty

The gardens were sold in 1948 to Mr. & Mrs. Albert Corbett (deceased) by Mrs. Sadie Pope, daughter of Mrs. Walters and Mr. Jones, and is presently owned by Mr. & Mrs. Waddell Corbett.

Georgie Hurst Franks, *A Brief History of the Wrightsville Beach Sound Community* (Courtesy of Joe Bennett)

The Support System

Trusted servants were a key element in the Joneses' lifestyle. Lack of an income tax system and a pitifully low wage scale for "help" made the excesses of the gilded age possible. However, evidence suggests that the Joneses were more generous than most employers and that their steady, dependable staff had a place in their hearts. In 1903, Sarah and Pembroke Jones took black Airlie manager Joseph Lofton to Newport in an effort to reward "a faithful servant," an unheard of tribute in that era.[76]

Much of the affection was based on the intimate situation between servants and employers. Seldom were all servants out of earshot. They knew the peculiarities, fetishes, strengths, weaknesses and appetites of those for whom they worked. It was much better and safer to get and keep good help. If you could establish a pleasant banter with great economy of word, all the better. "The help knows a lot about a household. They ever more do," said a wise elderly Wilmingtonian.

Sons of the employees formed a boys' choir, led by adults in their churches. Their performances delighted the Joneses and Henry Walters, who would toss $5 and $10 gold pieces to the vocalists. At Christmas, the employers gave bountiful gifts to the servants, including fine clothing and jewelry. Years later, when daughter Sadie Pope closed the house at Airlie after Mrs. Walters's death, she gave many treasures, including Tiffany lamps, to the help. [77]

The employees even put their thoughts to music:

"I'm going to live until I die, die, die-es
White folks are living mighty high, high, high-h-h
Now sticks and stones may break my bones
But you can't break Mr. Pembroke Jones,
I'm gonna live anyhow until I dies."[78]

Most of the Airlie employees lived at MacCumber Station, a trolley stop away. Pembroke Jones deeded them land on which they built frame homes. They also constructed churches on land donated by the Joneses: St. Matthew's African Methodist Episcopal Church, built in 1881, and the Pilgrim Rest Baptist Church, built in 1908. The churches still stand and have active congregations.

Just east of the churches was a two-room school, Wrightsville Sound School, where Miss Annie Webber and Miss Carrie Lane taught neighborhood black children. Miss Carrie Lane was born in 1874. Her mother had been a slave in the Bradley household. Miss Lane was a graduate of Scotia Seminary, in Concord, N. C. In addition to working at Peabody School, she taught at Williston Primary School. A founder of the Phyllis Wheatley branch of the Y.W.C.A., she died in 1981, at the age of 108. There was a baseball field across the street, where the Galleria Shopping Center now stands. The school building was destroyed by fire October 19, 1992.[79]

In the 1920s and 30s, when cars became more commonplace, several blacks were killed by cars speeding by MacCumber Terrace. Wrightsville Beach resident Richard Meier worked at Johnson Motor Works and was the salesman who provided cars for the Walterses. He knew many of the servants and notified state officials. The speed limit was lowered and the accidents ended.

Eugene Hurst, Evelena Bernard, Maria Mandy, Jessie Bertha DeBurneir, Margaret Mack, George Evans, Minnie Evans, Julius Evans, Beulah Franks, Mable Mack, Mary Mack, Mary Anna Smith, Ralph James Smith, Rachel Green Campbell, Rachel Green, Millie Mack, Preston Mack, Josephine Steadman, Charlie Whitty and many others worked at Airlie. Thomas A. Tartt, a gardener, began working at Airlie in 1915 and continued until his death in 1977. "This paradise," the employees called Airlie.[80]

Unlike the others, Minnie and Julius Caesar Evans lived at Pembroke Park where they could keep watch on the Lodge. Today, the gates of Airlie still remind many natives of their former keeper: artist Minnie Evans, whose interpretations of Airlie's flora and fauna have been shown in the Museum of Modern Art in New York, the Portal Gallery in London and several Parisian galleries. Writers like Nathan Comfort Starr have been frustrated searching for the origin of the Oriental "strain" in Mrs. Evans's art. If one looked hard enough, there was Eastern influence, both at Airlie, and at Pembroke Park.

Minnie Evans, who dressed up the world in her paintings, sits here unadorned, except for the glow of wisdom. This photograph, taken by Nina Howell Starr, appeared in *Painting Dreams: Minnie Evans, Visionary Artist*, written by Mary E. Lyons, in 1996. Through the years, Minnie Evans greeted thousands of visitors to Airlie. The prudent ones bought a painting along with their ticket. (Photo-Researchers, New York City)

Minnie Evans became an artist at least thirteen years before she became the gatekeeper at Airlie, in 1948. It's tempting to speculate on the sources of her inspiration. She herself said that it all came from within, which is true. However, external influences impress the mind. There is no doubt her creativity was inborn. She had been dreaming artwork since she was a child. Colorful stories passed down from her grandmother about their ancestors' origins in Africa and a stay in Trinidad fueled her hearty imagination. Tales of slavery, abuse, and relocation were recited even after she and her mother moved to Wrightsville Sound. Ella Jones Kelly and daughter Minnie Jones were "gatherers," workers who plucked bushels of oysters from the waters and took them into Wilmington to sell. Mrs. Kelly was known as "Hon" to close friends, a name that originated in childhood because of her sweet disposition. According to Minnie's biographer, Mary E. Lyons, Minnie loved working with her mother on the Sound, even though she earned only $2.50 a week.

In 1908, when Minnie was only fifteen, she met Julius Caesar Evans, an employee of Pembroke Jones. Evans worked at Pembroke Park and served as one of twenty coachmen when Jones's guests were in town. He dressed in tails and wore a high hat and was very popular with the visitors because of his easygoing congenial personality. After she turned sixteen, Minnie and Julius were married in Evans's green, five-room house, about 300 yards from the

Lodge at Pembroke Park. Beginning in 1910, they had three boys, Elisha, David and George, spaced five years apart. In the fashion of old plantation owners, Pembroke Jones named the babies. He chose names of some of his best friends. Elisha was named for Elisha Dyer, son of Rhode Island Governor Elisha Dyer. David was possibly named for a member of the Rockefeller family. Youngest son George Evans was named for George Vanderbilt, owner of Biltmore Estate in Asheville. "I started working at Airlie as a footman (and house servant) when I was eleven years old. I must have been eleven: by my 12th birthday, I was already here," said Mr. Evans at Airlie, in 2001.

In addition to family responsibilities, she took on many jobs at Pembroke Park, eventually becoming head house servant. One of the perks of her job was giving parties for her friends soon after parties had been hosted at the Lodge. The Joneses supplied the food, surplus from their banquets, and spare decorations were used to brighten the Evanses' house. Many of the friends who attended Minnie Evans's parties were members of Minnie's beloved church, St. Matthew's African Methodist.

Detail of rug (Parke Bernet Galleries, Inc., Art Collection of Mrs. Henry Walters, Part I.)

When their employer was in residence there was little time to reflect. However, the majority of the time, the Lodge was empty, giving the Evanses a 2200-acre "yard" and Minnie a few more leisure moments. The dark woods, the Oriental land-scaping adjacent to the oyster roast and the artwork contained in the Lodge must have had their influence. Oriental rugs contain-ing mystical symbols abounded. There was not one cultivated bloom at Pembroke Park, but its natural beauty was said to surpass that of Airlie. Perhaps the origins of her statement, "There are 2000 shades of green in God's palette,"come from years of observing the homogeneous botanical life at Pembroke Park.[81]

Minnie and Julius Evans spent more time in Jones's grand getaway than any of the other servants. Surely as she carried out her duties as head housekeeper, Minnie Evans studied the fascinating array of art Henry Walters had assembled for his best friends. We know that Sarah Jones Walters owned Chinese carvings, bronzes, porcelains, fig-urines, panoramic paintings, embroidered robes, prints; Persian rugs full of mystical figures; and Japanese prints. Perhaps the Lodge and the park in all its woodsy fullness contributed mystically to the creative epiphany Minnie Evans experienced while living there. One way or the other, in 1935, Minnie Evans became an artist while living at the edge of Mr. Jones's forest.

In 1999, George Evans was asked what his father, Julius, thought about his mother's artwork. He responded, "He was just like everybody else. He thought he had lost her. He thought she was going crazy. She went into some sort of trance before she went into painting. You see, she was given this talent three times before she would take it. The first two times, she laughed about it. She would tell us about it.

"So a third time this happened. I used to know what night it was. We were all there. Anyway, it was about two o'clock in the morning and God came to her and waked her up and lit up one side of her room and stood in the light and talked to her and said, 'Minnie, you're going to do these pictures or die.' And she came out of that room screaming and hollering."

Then she began to paint. How sad that Henry Walters, the consummate art lover, did not live to see Minnie Evans's metamorphosis. She was the artist right under his nose.[82]

Evans continued to paint from her dreams and daydreams, even into old age. Thomascenia Toney McKoy, a caregiver for Minnie and Minnie's mother in her last years, said: "Her pictures came from her dreams, whether they were good or some kind of nightmare. One day Minnie drew a picture," said Mrs. McKoy, "and she drew a wheel in the air. I asked her why and she said that she dreamed the picture the night before and in her dream, the wheel was in the air, so she *drew* the wheel in the air."

As Wrightsville Sound historian J. Fred Newber said, "The gatekeeper's art came to us from the heart and soul."[83]

The Corbett family hired Minnie Evans to manage the ticket booth at Airlie in 1948. Doubtless the flower gardens influenced the color and content of her work after that time, and she painted a number of works that she named "Airlie." In her early days as gatekeeper, Julius was not far away. The Corbett family hired him to be, according to his son George, "the Old Man of Airlie." Once again, Julius Evans donned a top hat and tails, but this time as a guide. He told visitors to Airlie interesting and amusing stories about his days working for the Jones and Walters families. The tourists were delighted.

Meanwhile, Minnie continued to paint. Not everyone who saw her work was complimentary. Some people even laughed. Finally, in 1961, a student in fine art photography, Nina Howell Starr, recognized Minnie Evans's talent after a friend showed her five of Evans's paintings. Distracted by the vivid colors, Starr photographed the paintings using black and white film. When she examined the resulting prints, Starr was awed by the design and balance of the work. She traveled to Wilmington in 1962 to meet the artist and to begin a series of taped interviews that would go on until 1973. Nina Starr began promoting and marketing Evans's work, placing it in New York galleries. In August 1969, Newsweek wrote of Minnie Evans, calling her a "beautiful dreamer." The price of her work began to climb, and more art authorities took notice. By the time she died, in 1987, she was a famous artist whose paintings brought as much as $15,000.[84]

Minnie and Julius Evans's son, George (center), poses at Mount Lebanon with his four sons (left to right), Rodney, George Jr., Gary and Norris, September 9, 2001. George's parents, Minnie and Julius Evans, were present at the Jones-Russell wedding. By age eleven, George worked for the Walterses on the Airlie estate. (Susan Block)

Many of the employees' names have been lost over the years, but usually the staff numbered about fifty. As George Evans said, "Mrs. Walters would look at all of us and smile and say, 'I'm the mother of Wrightsville Sound.'"

"Mrs. Jones is of medium height, with a figure neither plump nor slight, dark brown hair and eyes. She is noted for her unassuming and cordial manners and is extremely popular," noted the Wilmington *Messenger*, February 4, 1906. She is pictured here, in Newport. (Brown Brothers)

Movin' On Up

At the close of the 19th century, Sarah and Pembroke Jones, children of the Old South, were making a rapid social ascent "up North." They added a fine new residence to their personal address book, 13 West 51st Street, in New York, and took the advice of Pembroke's friend, socialite Henry Lehr, who told them to feed their guests well and often. The Joneses had some of their best Southern cooks on hand, as well as the services of a Russian chef. Their guests included many of New York's richest and most sophisticated residents who were regaled with warmth, wit, a lavish bar, and sumptuous food laden with fat grams. True to Sarah Jones's style of entertaining, things were not so ostentatious as they were simply grand.

The following year, newspaper reports of their whereabouts increased. The press announced that Sarah and Pembroke had created a sort of social coup in Newport, as well, where they leased a cottage called Friedheim. "The obtaining of a place in Newport society is more or less of a lottery," said a reporter for *New York World*, in September 1899. "Many attempts are made but the majority are more or less of a failure. Few gain prominence so quickly as the Pembroke Joneses."[85]

Sarah and Pembroke purchased Friedheim in 1908 and renamed it Sherwood, a name prominent among Jones's ancestors. They transformed it, with the help of architects Hoppin, Koen and Huntington, into a Georgian revival residence. As usual the Joneses added their hospitable signature, an eye-catching entryway, but this time it resembled the portico at the White House. Expansion and added flair allowed them to entertain bejeweled crowds while showcasing art, antiques and the master's racing trophies. Sherwood still exists but has been turned into condominiums.[86]

In January 1901, a whirlwind of work began at Airlie in preparation for a visit by some of the Joneses' new friends. Laborers erected a large entertainment space that would be used as a ballroom, theater and an indoor tennis court. When the need arose for a banquet hall, the space was transformed and a dining table that could seat 80 was assembled. Hardwood floors, an arched ceiling, and peripheral spectator seats made the interior resemble a resort pavilion. Charles McMillen served as architect and C. T. Shepard, as contractor. Clarence Maffitt, a ships' chandler, shipping agent and Pembroke Jones's distant cousin, created a huge canvas to protect the floors when guests played tennis. Outdoors, Will Rehder created an "old fashioned" flower garden. The work went on, even as guests from the North poured into Airlie for a Lenten holiday, February 24 to March 15.[87]

Mary Lily Kenan became one of the world's wealthiest women after her marriage to another friend of the Joneses: Henry Flagler. Mrs. Flagler was godmother to Jane Pope Akers Ridgway. (Brown Brothers)

Two guests whom the Joneses saw frequently were Mary Lily Kenan and Henry Flagler. The Joneses and the Kenans were family friends, and Sarah Jones and Mary Lily had known each other since childhood. Additionally, Henry Walters and Flagler were close business friends, sharing railroad interests and stockbrokers. Sarah Jones introduced Mary Lily to Henry Flagler, second only to John D. Rockefeller in Standard Oil shareholdings. An accomplished vocalist, Mary Lily gave several performances at Airlie for the Joneses and their other guests.

Eleven days after Flagler divorced his first wife on newly legislated grounds of incurable insanity, he married the 34-year-old Presbyterian, on August 24, 1901, in a service at Liberty Hall in Kenansville. Henry Walters was present, but many friends of the Kenan family opted not to attend the controversial nuptials. Those who declined were mostly members of Wilmington's First Presbyterian Church, stalwart souls of Scots blood who thought Mr. Flagler had tampered a bit with his own predestination. The tolerance of friends in attendance was rewarded: Standard Oil stock certificates rested under each guest's reception plate. The same stock, now in different forms, still exists in the portfolios of several Wilmingtonians.

In 1902, the Sarah Jones estate expanded significantly when she purchased property adjacent to Airlie, from C. S. Grainger. Shaped roughly like a triangle, it encompassed what we know today as Airlie Lake and extended down Airlie Road almost to the present-day entrance. A parcel purchased from the Edward Latimer family provided the land where the gate now stands. In time, Sarah Walters bought other choice waterfront tracts from neighbors H. C. McQueen and Warren G. Elliott, former president of the Wilmington and Weldon Railroad. The new acquisitions were part of the other half of the 1736 royal land grant, known by 1804 as Sedge Field on the Sound. When Mrs. Jones purchased it, she became the first person since Jonathan and Solomon Ogden to own a majority of the grant. Eventually, her holdings on the sound included property north of Airlie Road, purchased from the Giles, McGowan, Louisa Wright and Powell families.[88]

In January 1902, contractor F. R. Applegate and 25 carpenters and workmen from Wilmington began creating handsome servants' quarters, carriage and cart houses, and stables at Airlie. The servants' quarters contained individual baths, a luxurious arrangement at the time. The stables, "the handsomest in the State," were fitted with built-in harness cabinets. Applegate also created the dams to make the lake possible. Prior to that, a sizable creek, "Church Creek," crossed Airlie Road and ran near Lebanon Chapel. Other small creeks were dammed as well. Once damming was complete, Applegate created a rustic foot bridge and a charming duck blind. A golf course was completed and plans made for a 1000-gallon steel water tank and a "commodious golf house."[89]

Another workman, an artisan who crafted the interiors of luxurious Pullman cars, worked at Airlie in those years. Accustomed to finely detailed work, Walter G. Hatch had many tasks at Airlie, often directed by telephone when Mrs. Jones was in New York or Newport. Customarily, she deposited ample funds in Mr. Hatch's bank account for labor, fees, and supplies with the agreement that he would return the balance to her. One day she called with news that she had purchased new wallpaper while in Paris, was sending it by rail and wanted Mr. Hatch to supervise the hanging. When it arrived, the contractor was amazed. Painted by two Chinese artists, the paper was covered in graceful garden images, no two shrubs or birds being exactly alike. After Mr. Hatch examined the paintings, he decided against merely hanging the paper. He called for hundreds of yards of canvas backing so the wallpaper wouldn't tear when removed. Today remnants of the wallpaper have been divided among members of the Corbett family. It retains its beauty.

Pembroke Jones, about 1915. (Cape Fear Museum)

Walter Hatch also learned to mix paints to please his exacting employer. Mrs. Jones, famous among the workmen for not making purchases in Wilmington, finally conceded that Mr. Hatch could mix paint as well as her New York supplier. "She wouldn't let anyone but Papa paint those wooden eagles on the gates. They had to be painted a certain shade of gray that she called 'my shade of gray.' Papa knew how to mix the gray into white so that the color pleased Mrs. Walters. She was a very forceful person with a hearty voice and she knew what she wanted." said Walter Hatch's grandson Fred, in 2001.

The Joneses and Henry Walters arrived from New York on February 20, 1902, with plans to remain at Airlie six to eight weeks. During their stay, they entertained Mr. and Mrs. Stuyvesant Fish, Mr. and Mrs. Henry Lehr, Mrs. John Drexel, Herman Oelrich, F. L. V. Hoppin, Mr. and Mrs. Francis Stevens, William Nielson, Mr. and Mrs. Norman Whitehouse, Mr. and Mrs. Sydney Smith, Phoenix Ingram, Mr. and Mrs. Townsend Burden and other "leading society folk of New York." The visitors boarded beach cars, reserved by Pembroke Jones, at Union Station and rode to Airlie Road in handsome horse-drawn carriages. Apparently, the Joneses' guests arrived and left happy.

"I remember people coming and going in carriages to Mr. Jones's parties. There was laughter, so much laughter, and sometimes they would sing beautifully," Minnie Evans told author Barbara Marcroft.[90]

Minnie's son, George Evans, born August 29, 1915, was only four years old when Jones died. However his boyhood memories retain something of Jones's personality. "He loved everybody, *every*body. You could hear him before you saw him - loud, friendly greetings.

"He had his horses and the carriages and he was a jolly man," said Evans. "He just loved entertaining and going around shaking hands with people. During Christmas time he would have his horse and buggy all dressed up and he would go all around through the neighborhood singing and hullaballooing and all that kind of thing."

Mamie Fish, wife of Illinois Central Railroad President Stuyvesant Fish, possessed a generous dose of sardonic wit. She entertained and quipped her way to the top of Newport society before falling a bit from favor when she dared invite actors to her parties. In addition to a palatial New York home, the Fishes built Crossways, a Newport mansion, near Bailey's Beach. Mrs. Fish was one of Airlie's most frequent guests.

Col. C. L. F. Robinson, Pembroke Jones, Elisha Dyer and Pembroke Jones III, in Newport. (Brown Brothers)

Though a schedule so full of social activities might make the average person run for solitary cover, it is undebatable that the Joneses and their guests enjoyed such occasions beyond measure. "Sometimes we would go down to Wilmington where Pembroke Jones dispensed hearty, southern hospitality," wrote one New York socialite. "We were bound to have a good time. Plenty of gaiety and laughter and fun...the welcome that awaited us was so real and the pleasure on our host and hostess's face so genuine and the enormous hot supper so good that we forgot the fatigue of the journey."[91]

Local papers announced regularly the arrivals and departures of the rich and famous who came to visit at Airlie.

Through the local press, Mrs. Jones kept open a narrow window on life at Airlie. Happy was the reporter fortunate enough to get an Airlie assignment. After 1906, Mrs. Jones began to rely on Louis T. Moore, a writer for the *Star News*, and later, executive secretary of the Chamber of Commerce, to publicize and promote. Moore, a descendant of "King" Roger Moore, owner of Orton Plantation, married Florence Kidder, sister of George Kidder, who was a close friend of the Jones and Kenan families and another frequent visitor to Airlie.[92]

The local press heralded the news when Cornelius Vanderbilt introduced the Joneses to Prince Henry of Germany, when Mrs. Jones had a private audience with Pope Pius X, when the Joneses took a boatful of guests down the river on the steamer *Wilmington*, and when 250 Princeton students spent their New Years holiday at Airlie, greeted by the Joneses and an elaborate fireworks display over the lake. Wilmingtonians were apprised of many of Henry Walters's art purchases: three fine works from the New York "Stewart Sale," the original handwritten version of "The Star Spangled Banner" by Francis Scott Key, and the Don Marcello Massarenti Collection, the art that became the core collection of the Walters Art Gallery.

Articles told of the Joneses' visits to the Flagler residence at Palm Beach and listed the winners of golf tournaments held at Airlie. The newspaper carried advertisements for scores of extra carriages for the Joneses' house parties. And most townspeople were amused when they read, "Mr. Pembroke Jones and a large party of his guests at Airlie drove up to the city yesterday from the sound. They came in a Tally-ho (a large, open horse drawn carriage with elevated seats) and drove about the city and the bugle blasts attracted much attention as the merry party saw the town."

But it was another activity that caused Pembroke Jones to expand his 155-acre tract to about 2355 acres. In 1901, visitors from New York and Newport were thrilled with a nighttime hunt at Airlie, conducted by moon and torchlight under thick canopies of silvery Spanish moss. Led by Airlie manager Joseph Lofton, a black man who was also a talented chef, the well-heeled guests rode handsome steeds through the lush Wrightsville Sound woods. Despite their attire they bagged mostly mundane game, the living party favors that were augmented by Pembroke Jones's staff months before the guests arrived. Mrs. Stuyvesant Fish shot a raccoon, an animal about as rare in New Hanover County soundfront communities as linen napkins were on Newport tables. But Mrs. Fish was thrilled and had the poor masked creature stuffed and mounted. For years, it graced a select space in her lavish Newport mansion, Crossways.

RESIDENCE OF PEMBROKE JONES, NEWPORT, R. I.

This photo, taken March 19, 1902, pictures members of the Wilmington Hunt Club at Pembroke Park. Those pictured are: Harry Solomon (boy), Ben Solomon (with mustache), Jacob Solomon (in cap, on white horse), Adolph Goodman (hat with brim, 3rd from right). (Miriam Solomon Baggett)

The Annex

In February 1902, Jones began purchasing property north of Airlie for a hunting preserve. He bought as if he were a Monopoly player with no opponent and he amassed it in his name, just as Airlie was solely the property of Mrs. Jones. At first, Thomas H. Wright acted as agent by buying outright tracts of land that he then sold to Pembroke Jones, sometimes the following day. Eventually, Wright took on a more traditional role as he brokered real estate transactions straight to Mr. Jones. The land acquisition game would go on until 1918, the year before Jones died, and would include a large number of sellers: Lord, Grainger, Walker, Poisson, Cameron, Price, Williams, Bradley, Newkirk, Bunting, Blue, Miller, Sidbury, Divine, James, Holly, Lillie and Craft.

The sprawling estate provided bounteous space and plenty of bounty for Jones's hunting friends. In November 1902, George Vanderbilt of Biltmore fame visited Airlie, preceded by a crack team of hunting dogs. Harry Lehr and William K. Vanderbilt joined in the pursuit, as well as a dozen other famous names. It was the beginning of a new era: Pembroke Jones's adventure world was on America's social map.

Though others altered the name, Mr. Jones first called the new tract "Pembroke Park at Airlie," and constructed a 28-mile shell road through it. Indeed it was originally an extension of Airlie, but with a quite masculine stamp. Though Mrs. Walters reigned at Airlie, Pembroke Park was the site of many stag parties and an elegant accommodation for house guests who spilled over from Airlie. Even the grounds were more masculine: In contrast to the sea of flowers at Airlie, Pembroke Park had wildflowers but not one cultivated blossom.[93]

Pembroke Jones made plans to build a rustic mail-order hunting cabin on a bluff overlooking the Sound but was discouraged by a friend. "You are losing a great opportunity for getting something just a little more expensive but ever so much more beautiful." John Stewart Barney (1869-1925), a frequent Airlie guest, was chosen as architect. Although a Richmond native, Barney had strong ties to New York. His family residence at 861 Lexington Avenue was occupied by Barneys from 1772 until the early 1990s. Pembroke Jones apparently met Barney in Newport. Mary Alice Van Nest Barney and Mrs. Jones shared a misfortune of privilege. They both had diamonds stolen while guests at the White Ball, an event hosted by Nevada silver heiress Mrs. Hermann Oelrichs in Newport. Rosecliff, Tessie Oelrichs's Newport mansion, was designed by architect Stanford White to resemble Le Grand Trianon, a palace in Versailles. Sarah Jones's jewel, part of a filigree pin made by Tiffany, was so magnificent that a facsimile was exhibited at the St. Louis Fair.

J. Stewart Barney's other architectural work included the restoration of Bruton Parish Church in Williamsburg (1907) and collaboration on designs for the Beaux Arts style Handley Regional Library in Winchester, Virginia; the Troy Memorial Library, in Troy, New York; the Emmet Building, Broadway Tabernacle, Hotel Navarre, the Rhinelander Memorial, the McAlpin-Fox House at the Cooper-Hewitt Museum, The Church of the Holy Trinity, and Grace Mission Complex in New York City. He was one of the first architects to advocate using vertical lines in skyscrapers. It was considered a radical idea because the Architectural League endorsed horizontal lines, thinking it best to camouflage the extreme height of the buildings.[94]

Architect J. Stewart Barney in his office, about 1905. (Stewart Barney Kean)

Once a partner of New York mansion architects Henry Otis Chapman and C. P. H. Gilbert, J. Stewart Barney was acquainted with many wealthy clients and networked with a web of New York architects, including Kenneth M. Murchison. Murchison, who was the brother of Wilmingtonian Luola M. Sprunt, distinguished himself as a designer of railroad depots, most notably at Baltimore, Erie, Johnstown, Scranton, Hoboken and Jacksonville. J. Stewart Barney's former partner, Gilbert, designed Wilmington's Cape Fear Club, on the southeast corner of Second and Chestnut streets. It's difficult not to imagine that Henry Walters, who was the powerful chief executive of the Atlantic Coast Line Railroad, a member of the Cape Fear Club, and adhering mate to the Pembroke Joneses, did not do some weaving of the web.

About 1914, J. Stewart Barney wandered away from the drawing table to become an artist and sculptor. He moved to Paris where he studied watercolors and oils. His landscapes of Newport, Bar Harbor, and Scotland remain popular. In 1915 he published a novel, *L. P. M.: The End of the Great War*, that gives glimpses into the lives of the privileged, including a wealthy, well-connected couple named Jones. Perhaps Barney drew on memories of the *Narada* when he wrote the following description. If so, both the *Narada* and Walters's Pullman car gave the illusion of being a not-so-ordinary homes.

"He was in a parlour or sitting room, about fifteen by twenty, neatly but handsomely furnished. Nothing about it indicated that it was ever off an even keel. There were no racks or other contrivances to suggest that it was prepared to turn in any direction at an angle of 45 degrees. It might indeed have been a handsome living-room in a bachelor's apartment, but for the windows, which at the first glance seemed to be of the ordinary French casement form, running down to the floor, and looking as if they might open out onto a balcony; but to his surprise, he found, when he pulled aside the heavy curtains, that they looked into a perfectly blank wall about two inches from the glass."

In 1903, J. Stewart Barney designed an Italianate showplace for Pembroke Jones in which the doorknobs alone cost more than the owner's original plan, $1500. Two carpenters and a large crew of local laborers built the wood and stone masterpiece in a year at a cost of $50,000. When the house was complete, the Italian ambassador himself visited and declared it "the most perfect note of Italy in America." Writer Samuel Howe compared the building and setting to a scene straight out of a Maeterlinckian drama, particularly theater manager Oscar Hammerstein's (1847-1919) version of Debussy's "Pelleas et Melisande."

The Lodge at Pembroke Park, "The place is neither spoiled nor belittled by foolish subdivisions." — Samuel Howe, 1915 (Cape Fear Museum)

The interior was stunning: three adjoining great rooms with multivaulted ceilings, many elaborately furnished apartments in one wing and a kitchen fit to cater hundreds of guests in the other. The great hall, capped by a high multivaulted ceiling, sported two large Italian Renaissance stone mantels, each of which was supported by two carved female nudes. The walls of the apartments were divided into panels by Ionic columns in bas-relief. Indirect lighting and a simple air conditioning system added a touch of the future to the old-world charm.

The kitchen was large enough to contain a complete bakery, and the butler's pantry held a gold and silver service for two hundred. A trapdoor led to a wine cellar. The ceiling of the immense dining room was solid and vaulted, but natural light often bathed the room. The light came from an adjoining solarium that featured a glass ceiling, augmented throughout with fine black wire. Electricity had reached Airlie and Pembroke Park in 1903, making both properties dazzling against the night sky. For more tranquil guests, the black walnut library beckoned. A handful of Wilmingtonians still remember the handsome space, particularly one detail: One of the walnut panels, though uniform in appearance, was actually a door leading to a bedroom.

The house was furnished with items from an Italian palace, including a large collection of elaborate painted chests. In 1902, Henry Walters purchased all the contents of Palazzo Accoramboni, in Rome, for $1 million. What better way to display a portion of them than to build a little Italian palace in America? It was filled with contents so different from anything else in southeastern North Carolina that well-spoken eyewitnesses still have trouble describing it. The local tradition that "it was Henry Walters's money" probably holds true for the Lodge, a premise substantiated by the lack of publicity during and after the Lodge's construction.

Outside, facing Wrightsville Sound, an old Gatling gun was mounted on the terrace, close to a stone lily pool with Goliath-size goldfish, about 10' by 6', lined with mirror tile. A bridge nearby matched the style of the Lodge. Between the house and Wrightsville Sound, in the midst of a grove of oaks, pines, and magnolias, there was an imposing bronze statue of Cupid. A 1000-gallon tank fed water to the house, about 500 feet away, through a two-inch pipe.[95]

This photo, taken after the Lodge was abandoned, reveals a portion of the pool between the house and Wrightsville Sound. Numerous bronze turtles like the ones seen here, spewed water at the goldfish. The Gatling gun in the background boomed when Pembroke Jones partied. (Lossie Gardell, St. Andrew's on-the-Sound)

Capriciously arranged coquina terraces adorned the grounds around the Lodge, or Bungalow as it was called originally. They swirled in the shape of a warped "S," much like waves lapping on an uneven shore. Multilength contoured steps made of moss-covered ground and green creeper dodged roots and tree trunks. The terraces and steps rose at uneven but medium-range increments, but the terrace line on which the Lodge stood was straight and elevated a full five feet.

Beyond the terraced lawn, on the opposite side of the house, sat the Temple of Love, designed by John Russell Pope, a famous architect who, in 1912, would marry Sadie Jones, daughter of Sarah and Pembroke Jones. Mr. Pope spent the last few years of the 19th century studying architecture in France, Greece and Italy, and later joined the architectural firm of McKim, Mead and White, well known to the Joneses. The Temple of Love, according to Pope's biographer, Stephen Bedford, was the first in a series of buildings spun from this design that culminated in his most famous American creation: the Jefferson Memorial. Pope also designed the NSDAR Constitution Hall, National Archives building and American Institute of Natural History, in Washington, D. C.; and Richmond's Broad Street Station, now the Virginia Science Museum; many structures for the Vanderbilt family, including the Trianon Inn and 12 toll lodges on the Long Island Motor Parkway, The Breakers, in Newport, and the Virginia Vanderbilt House, in New York; the Marshall Field residence, "Caumsett," on Long Island, now a state park; and Skylands, a private residence that is now a New Jersey state park.[96]

In Wilmington, John Russell Pope designed in 1915 a house for Elliotte Emerson and Albert Sidney Williams, at 102 North 15th Street. Located next door to the home of Thomas H. Wright, developer of Carolina Heights, the house sits on two lots once owned by Pembroke Jones.

At Pembroke Park, the coquina gazebo was the centerpiece of the Joneses' Temple of Love. It canopied a small fountain ornamented by a bronze reproduction of Andrea del Verrocchio's 1470 Florentine sculpture, *Putto with Dolphin*. The six-columned gazebo was surrounded by a circle made of four wedge-shaped pools that were connected by walkways. Each pool held a different kind of fresh fish for the dining pleasure of Jones's guests, some of whom "caught" their catch with a crab net. Julius and George Evans emptied and cleaned the pools twice a year, protecting the fish in huge enamel tubs until fresh water in the pools reached the correct temperature.

John Russell Pope designed the Temple of Love, at Pembroke Park. The architect "seemed to adhere to the precept that a certain set of classical forms and plans existed whose inherent beauty was immutable," said Pope's biographer, Stephen McLeod Bedford. (Lower Cape Fear Historical Society)

Coquina for the gazebo and pools was made by mixing concrete with a variety of shells from Wrightsville Sound. In 1915, architect Samuel Howe wrote, "Of course, the temple is white, but not the white of Italy's statuary marble nor the polished equivalent from some neighboring state, but following the precedent of the great craft workers of the Renaissance, local materials have been exclusively used. Here is the oldest and newest form of building material."[97]

John Russell Pope (*John Russell Pope: Architect of Empire* by Steven McLeod Bedford)

In 1915, rustic gates that created the boundary between Airlie and Pembroke Park were replaced by new ones, designed by John Russell Pope. Architectural historian Samuel Howe called the classical entrance, "an agreeable surprise." Banked in dark green cedar and hemlock, the masonry gates, painted in white and silvery gray, created a pleasant contrast that could be seen from a distance. When visitors, particularly those in fancy dress, drew closer, they could see another contrast. The gates feature scenes, created in low relief, of an ancient chariot race, in which participants are dressed in nature's simplest attire.

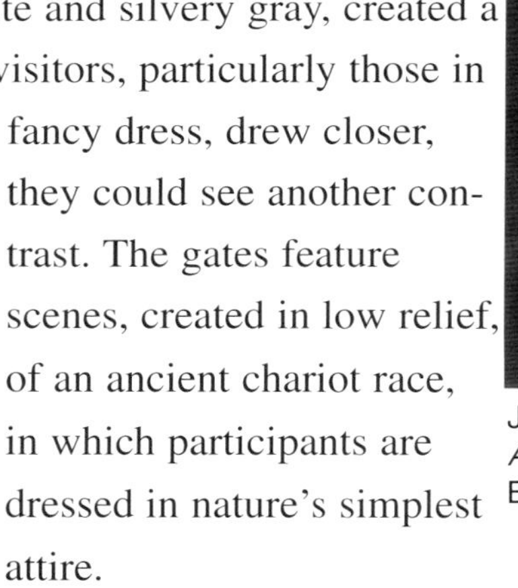

John Russell Pope's classical entrance divided Airlie and Pembroke Park. (Wrightsville Beach Magazine)

There were also watering troughs for the birds and vases that held fresh arrangements when parties were held. Each gate was topped by a statue of a lion crushing a serpent. "The entrance is a timely promise of the beauties within the boundary," said Mr. Howe. The same could be said whether one was traveling north or south. The road south from the gates led down Jones Road, just west of the churches at MacCumber Station, then wound east of St. Andrew's on-the-Sound, toward the existing Airlie gate.

Sometimes at Pembroke Park, Jones's capricious nature exhibited itself fully. Third-generation Wrightsville Sound resident Jane Holman Hardwick grew up hearing tales of parades of fine carriages passing along the old ballast stone surface of Summer Rest Road, as the Joneses' guests arrived for parties, the most famous being the "Tree Party." Airlie superintendent W. C. Taylor, interviewed by Lewis Philip Hall, concurred. His own father, W. A. Taylor (1868-1947) oversaw plans for the event, one that married Southern hospitality and Wrightsville Sound's ancient, sprawling live oaks.

On that occasion, the Joneses' guests traveled toward a surreal holiday where classical musicians and adventuresome guests climbed freshly cut gently spiraling stairs to platforms in the giant live oaks. White linen and sterling silver graced the tables as fireflies lit up the night. Peter Hill, the same man who delivered ice to the Joneses when they lived at 400 South Front Street, brought ice to Pembroke Park. Mr. Hill and his helpers placed 200-pound blocks of ice on the lawn to cool the guests.

On another occasion, Pembroke Jones's big city connections and knowledge of downtown Wilmington came together. One evening, the after-dinner entertainment at the Lodge was a private concert by Enrico Caruso. Caruso's pianist was ill, so Pembroke Jones engaged Mildred Kornegay, a pianist at the Bijou Theater, to accompany the world-famous tenor.[98]

Henry Walters (facing camera, with goatee) and friends enjoy an oyster roast at Pembroke Park, about 1905. (Lower Cape Fear Historical Society)

Though Sarah Jones was known to refer to the house at Airlie as the "fishing shack," it is not to be confused with "The Shack," a beloved structure that served as the site of hundreds of oyster roasts. "I remember the oyster roasts distinctly," said Eleanor Wright Beane. "We all rode from Airlie to the Lodge together. It was fun and there were always lots of oysters and lots of johnny cakes." Once inside Pembroke Park, the shell road, by design, twisted and turned, climbed and descended, until it reached the arrow-straight approach to the Lodge. Uniformly manicured ivy bordered the entire drive through Pembroke Park, just as it did at Airlie.

"They'd roast the oysters," of the famous New River variety, said another frequent guest, Rosalie Watters Carr. "They'd really roast them like they should be done. You could or could not have them opened for you. Some people preferred to open their own. Everybody had dessert after an oyster roast, something with lemons or lime, a citrus something."

Gabrielle Gibbs Holmes Willard is a Wilmingtonian whose ancestors, the Fleemings and the Gibbses, lived on Wrightsville Sound in the 1800s. "Citrus was considered rare in Wilmington," said Gibbs Willard. "Not native to the area, it had to be brought by rail and there was no refrigeration to keep it fresh. It was considered such a treat that children would be happy to find oranges in their Christmas stockings. So if the Joneses served good quality citrus, their oyster roasts ended on a special note," she said.

The Joneses' road that led to the Lodge wound around to the rustic log building. The Shack contained two wall-to-wall fireplaces used for oyster roasts. Pine needles scented with Cape Jessamine and India hawthorn served as a floor. When guests had had enough of oysters and johnnie cakes, they could slip away to a nearby lake and gaze at moonlit waters from a swinging Japanese bridge made of very small logs.

Just as guests from near enjoyed the Shack, so did many from afar. Pembroke Jones entertained the most notable gathering of large railroad owners ever assembled, at Airlie: Mr. William K. Vanderbilt, Jr., principal owner of the New York Central Railway, known as the Vanderbilt lines; Mr. A. H. Smith, president of the New York Central; Mr. Henry Walters, John R. Kenly and Mr. Lyman Delano, officers of the Atlantic Coast Line Railroad; and Mrs. H. M. Flagler, owner of the Florida East Coast Railway. Other guests: Mrs. Warren Delano, sister of Mr. Walters; Mr. David Barnes, a prominent member of the NY Stock Exchange. They came for oyster roasts, then departed on trains, Vanderbilt to Florida for a fishing trip, the others to the north.

Actually William Vanderbilt, Jr., (1878-1944) visited Airlie frequently, often arriving on his yacht, the *Tarantula*. Built in 1902 by the British navy as a torpedo boat, the *Tarantula* did not pass government inspection. Mr. Vanderbilt purchased and upgraded the vessel, then customized it luxuriously. "It is a speedy vessel, has every appearance of a torpedo boat and is said to be able to make between 25 and 30 knots an hour," said a *Star News* reporter, in 1909. "Captain A. E. Harding, the master, who is well known at this port, is in command.[99]

In 1912, Vanderbilt replaced the *Tarantula* with a similar one and christened it with the same name. This second *Tarantula*, built at Neponset, Mass., by George Lawley and Son Corp., also became government property when the U. S. Navy purchased it on April 25, 1917. She operated off the coast of Connecticut, New York, and New Jersey until October 1918, when she sank eight miles southwest of the Fire Island light after colliding with a Royal Holland Lloyd Line vessel. In April 1933, Vanderbilt docked at Southport on the *Alva*, his elegant ocean-going steam yacht.

Wilmington resident Robert Bridgers, grandson of railroad luminary R. R. Bridgers who attended the Joneses' wedding, remembers seeing one of the grand yachts that brought guests to Airlie. "They anchored it at Southport because it was too large to dock at Wilmington. Our whole family drove down to see it. It was a beautiful steam yacht. The crowd from New York sailed here occasionally, but mostly they came in private Pullman cars. Sometimes they would ride from Airlie to Pinehurst for the Southern Open.The train made a stop in Aberdeen. They were all fans of a Scottish golfer named Bobby Cruikshank."[100]

One day, years later, when Vanderbilt arrived at the Market Street dock, his trip to Wrightsville Sound was a little different from the usual. Executive Director of the Wilmington Chamber of Commerce Louis T. Moore received a telephone call from Mrs. Walters, prior to the railroad executive's arrival. "Could you greet my old friend, Willie Vanderbilt, when he arrives on his yacht at the Custom House?" Mr. Moore, always armed with some new historical facts gleaned from his never-ending research, gave Vanderbilt a customized tour before delivering him to the big white house at Airlie.[101]

William Vanderbilt's yacht, the *Alva* (Vanderbilt Museum)

The Toast of the Town

From 1901 through 1912, life at Airlie continued as Wilmington's nod to the Gilded Age, particularly during the Lenten season and the Christmas and New Year's holidays. Wilmingtonians mingled with guests from the North at dances, plays and golf matches at Airlie. Dolores Holt, wife of Edwin C. Holt, principal stockholder in Delgado Mills, won a few golf tournaments. So did Wilmington attorney George Rountree. In April 1904, Jones invited almost every member of Cape Fear Country Club to play at Airlie.

Sometimes, for holiday parties, the mile-long drive into Airlie was illuminated with Japanese lanterns and burning tar barrels. Wilmingtonians Hanna Bolles, Mr. and Mrs. William A. Dick, the Emersons, Clayton Giles, Jr., Tallulah deRosset, Cynthia Rountree, Florence Kidder, Agnes McQueen, Julia Worth, Norwood Huske, H. D. W. Rapalje, Elizabeth Bridgers, Haughton James, Meares Harriss, Wallace Carmichael, S. M. Boatwright, Burke Bridgers, Raymond Hunt, Elizabeth Bridgers, Janie Crowley and Isabel Smallbones were frequent visitors when Sarah and Pembroke Jones's daughter was in residence. Sadie Jones, an aspiring actress in her youth, was the creative force behind plays staged during that era at Airlie under the auspices of the Airlie Dramatic Club. Sadie's career choice did not delight her parents or her "Uncle Harry." *Town Topics* recorded the domestic scene: "In vain Mr. Jones threatens. In vain Mrs. Jones implores. In vain Mr. Walters advises. Sadie is obdurate." The problem would right itself soon enough.[102]

After guests had spent several days on the Sound, excursions into Wilmington broke the beautiful monotony. The Joneses rented a steamer, the *Atlantic*, in 1907, and took Mrs. Stuyvesant Fish, the Delanos (Henry Walter's sister's family) and a large number of New Yorkers to Orton Plantation and the vine-wrapped ruins of St. Philip's Church in Brunswick Town. Pembroke Jones's Wilmington friends had a different experience: Messrs. Wright, Emerson, Kenly, McIlhenny, Martin, McQueen, Rountree and Dr. Thomas sailed to Narragansett Bay on the *Narada* several times, including a trip where they witnessed from the yacht off Newport News, May 25, 1912, the launching of the battleship *Texas*.

The residence at Airlie expanded as Mrs. Jones's hospitable nature dictated. When complete, it took four heating plants to keep the house warm in winter. As George Evans said, in 1999, "She just kept developing and developing and developing." Eventually, she added thirty-eight apartments for guests. Most of the suites were reserved for a certain guest or couple. One of the visitors wrote in 1915: "Additions have been made and wings thrown out here and there until it is a house of many mansions. The roofs of Airlie, with their many angles and corners, suggest all manner of surprises and ramblings, and the interior does not belie the promise. You never get to the end of such a house. There is always a new room, or a passage leading to unknown territory. One might live there for a week and never guess that there was a covered tennis court right in the middle of the house."[103]

Exclusive of the indoor tennis courts and apartments, Airlie House was still enormous. There were twelve bedrooms: four on the first floor and a master suite and eight more bedrooms on the second. Other spaces included a library, writing room, dining room, coat room, office, ballroom, flower room (the solarium), house servants' quarters, a pressing room, pantry, and various richly furnished alcoves. In a time when party lines were prevalent, Airlie had the first private residential line in New Hanover County and its own telephone room. Mahogany furniture prevailed throughout, although there were some fine maple pieces in the master suite. The Joneses' own bed was made of bamboo shaped mahogany. The servants' bedrooms featured painted or stained oak furniture and enamel beds. At the bottom of the stairs in the basement, there was a room where saddles were stored.[104]

The appointments throughout the house were stunning. Eighteenth- and nineteenth-century heirlooms from Mrs. Jones's family were scattered among thousands of square feet of global treasures collected by Henry Walters and the Joneses. All arrived in Wilmington by train. Gilded chairs, priceless porcelains, sculpture, paintings, antique beds, Roman bronze lamps, a Tiffany grandfather clock and a Louis XV parquetry inlaid tulipwood writing desk graced Airlie. So did a 1731 sterling silver chalice, a George II silver teapot, a Venetian glass chandelier and a framed letter signed by George Washington on December 16, 1783. The flatware ranged from heavy, ornate pieces to the stylized forms of Georg Jensen.

Several sterling silver pieces engraved "E.S.G.," that once belonged to Sarah Jones Walters's mother, Esther Sargent Ellery Green, were displayed prominently. Exquisite miniatures, favorites of Henry Walters, punctuated spaces throughout the house. A bronze plaque hung on the office wall, saluting Mr. Walters's loan of the *Narada* to the U. S. Government in 1917. There were also two framed certificates from the New York Yacht Club.[105]

The majority of the framed art at Airlie was by Currier and Ives. However, other works included a painting of "The Yacht Dauntless of New York," Durer's "Knight in Armor Leaning" and "Head of Man," Barlow's "The Head of Washington," and Brown's "Gathering for the Meet." Outside there were bronze sculptures of two deer.[106]

The main ballroom had plenty of room for dancing despite the elegant writing desks scattered about, Chippendale side chairs, gilded chairs, stuffed wing chairs, and 30 tables, most of them mahogany, but some made of black lacquer. There were also two pianos, one square and one upright. Rolled carpets were stored nearby, cut to fit the ballroom floor if the owners so desired. Fine Kurd and Bokhara area rugs were used elsewhere at Airlie.

The commodious Airlie pantry was protected by multiple locks. "Mrs. Walters didn't let anyone else near those keys," said Fred Hatch, who met her several times when he was a boy. After Mrs. Walters died, inventory records indicate that Airlie qualified as an alcohol depot. Much of it came straight from the Walters family distillery business. Among many other spirits, there were 636 bottles of Baltimore rum, 168 bottles of Burnett's gin and hundreds of gallons of other liquors. There were also 144 bottles of "Baker's Pure, 1863" and 6 precious bottles of champagne, dated 1840.[107]

The Joneses owned many hundreds of rare volumes, most with elaborate gilt bindings, and assorted valuable documents. A short sampling includes George Washington's copy of M. T. Cicero's *Cato Major*, a work by Torquato Tasso bearing the gilded arms of Louis XVIII, Henry VIII's copy of Rosate's *Vocabularius*, two volumes owned by Napoleon Bonaparte, 41 original tracts by Martin Luther, the marriage contract signed by Louis XVI and Marie Antoinette and a book that had belonged to Lord Byron containing his handwritten comments. Like so many material elements of the Joneses' world, the book collection bears the illusionary fingerprints of Henry Walters, even to the number of volumes on armor, one of Mr. Walters's favorite collectibles.

The library at Airlie alone contained over 1500 books. There were volumes on collecting Chinese pottery, a history of English furniture, works by Hugo and Thackeray. Situated among the gilded first editions was a set of Britannica encyclopedias. For those who wanted to play games, there were backgammon and mah-jongg. Cigarette boxes were permanent features in the library as well as throughout the house. Cigarettes lay in monogrammed bronze, silver or jade boxes in the formal areas of the house.

In the year that Herbert and Empie Latimer were seniors at Princeton, the University Glee, Banjo and Mandolin clubs toured the East Coast, during the Christmas holidays. On December 25, 1907, 250 Princetonians arrived at the Atlantic Coast Line depot in Wilmington. Another train had wrecked near Raleigh, delaying their arrival in Wilmington until 9:30 at night. They were too late to attend the feast awaiting them at Luola and James Sprunt's house, at 400 South Front Street. The Sprunts' son, J. Laurence Sprunt, also was a student at Princeton and would graduate with the Class of 1910.[108]

The hungry boys performed at the Academy of Music (Thalian Hall) before boarding beach cars for Airlie. When they arrived, late on Christmas night, they were greeted by Sarah and Pembroke Jones and led to the ballroom for a "german." Young women from Wilmington and New York were present and the dance lasted for hours. Afterward, the college boys boarded beach cars again and headed for the streetcar stop at Front and Princess, just doors from their hotel, the Orton.

Airlie-on-the-Sound, as Mrs. Walters like to call it and as it was called until at least 1947, was filled to capacity again when the Joneses invited swarms of wedding guests in the fall of 1912. Though they had their choice of grand venues, Lebanon Chapel was chosen for the marriage of Sadie Green Jones, Sarah and Pembroke's only daughter, and architect John Russell Pope. Sadie's dreams of being an actress dissolved after she fell in love with the handsome architect. Pembroke Jones III and Lyman Delano, Mr. Walters's nephew, served as ushers. The Rt. Rev. Robert Strange, Dr. Thomas Henry Wright's grandson, performed the ceremony. He had also officiated at the wedding of the bride's parents in 1884.[109]

"Interest in local social circles has centered for some weeks in the wedding, and Baltimore, New York and Newport society was agog over the event," wrote one excited reporter. Though five hundred guests attended the reception at Airlie House, space dictated that only 100 could witness the exchange of vows in Lebanon Chapel. Smilax, white chrysanthemums and Easter lilies scented the air while the Conrad Orchestra of New York played Wagner, Mendelssohn and Grieg on a new organ and six stringed instruments. The rear pews were reserved for guests who probably knew Miss Jones well, "old family servants, Negroes who have always lived on the place."[110]

Photographer Charles Farrell took this photo of Airlie in the 1930s. (N. C. Division of Archives and History)

At the reception, "one of the most elaborate and brilliant... ever held in this part of the State," the newlyweds received guests under a bower of white roses in the dining hall. Sherry's, a New York caterer, served refreshments in the enclosed tennis court, which was draped in smilax garlands. Guests undoubtedly wondered where the privileged couple would honeymoon. However, it was not to be Venice or Rome. By 6:30, the bride and groom were on a train headed for an unnamed hunting preserve in the North Carolina mountains, "both being experts with the rifle."

"My mother was a strong person and her own person," said her daughter Jane Pope Akers Ridgway, 89 years later.

Sarah Jones, Pembroke Jones (back left) and Henry Walters (far right) did little posing for cameramen. This photograph, signed to Thomas H. Wright, from "PJ," was taken in California's Redwood Forest. (Eleanor Wright Beane)

All in the Extended Family

In 1913, the Joneses moved their New York residence from 13 West 51st Street to 5 East 61st Street. Though Henry Walters would leave for meetings in Baltimore, he usually returned to New York the same day, traveling in his handsome private railroad car. Henry Walters continued to live with Sarah and Pembroke Jones, an arrangement that raised a few eyebrows but not the dander of Pembroke Jones. William Johnston, author of *The Reticent Collectors: William and Henry Walters*, said it was reported that on one occasion at Airlie, Sarah Jones danced with Henry Walters while Pembroke Jones danced good-naturedly with the nanny.[111]

World War I brought changes to the Jones and Walters's household. Pembroke Jones made the 61st Street New York apartment available to the Royal Italian War Mission, but on November 15, 1916, the apartment was the site of a famous wedding: Mary Lily Kenan Flagler, now a widow, married Judge Robert Worth Bingham of Louisville, Kentucky. Jones had also become vice-president of the Carolina Shipbuilding Company, which made steel-hulled freighters. On May 26, 1918, he hosted a shipyard party at Airlie. Henry Walters, doing his share for the war effort, loaned the *Narada* to the U. S. Navy for tests of underwater listening equipment. Walters also lent the 51st Street apartment, having always been in his name, to the American Club as a shelter for women harmed economically by the war. Additionally, he supported a French military hospital in Passy. [112]

Sadly, Pembroke Jones died following surgery, January 25, 1919, at the age of 60, in New York City. His body arrived at Wilmington's Union Station two days later. After a funeral service at St. James Church, six black employees lovingly placed him in his grave at Oakdale Cemetery. Jones left instructions and a provision in his will to dedicate pew #49 "for the use of visitors who worship with us as a perpetual memorial to the aunt who reared him and was known by him as a mother, Mrs. Alice H. Dickinson."[113]

Sarah Jones married their friend Henry Walters in 1922, at her daughter's residence. "They made a little altar and we had the wedding in our home in New York," said Jane Pope Akers Ridgway, in 2001. It was the groom's first marriage. He was 74, she was 63. By that time, she was known for her booming voice. As always, he was on the quiet side.

Henry Walters was far better known to the Airlie servants than he was to any member of the press. Like Sarah and Pembroke Jones, he was loved by the help, a sterling tribute. "I can see him now with that white goatee. He always had a twinkle in his eye. Mr. Walters was an old man when I knew him. He had gout and a slight limp, but he'd smile that little smile. Henry Walters was very good to us," said George Evans.

Walters, whose personal economics did nothing to challenge the tradition of gout's being a "rich man's disease," fought it with turtle soup, made mostly from terrapins raised on his Maryland estate. "His employees cared for hundreds and hundreds of them," said Mr. Evans. "Then his cooks made soup from them - canned it and sent it to him by train wherever he was. He ate it twice a day, every day."

In the 1920s, the Bowden family on Summer Rest Road also raised terrapins on the porch of their Soundfront house. It is believed that some of the creatures made their way into Mr. Walters's soup as well.[114]

By the time the Walterses were married, Airlie had the look of a fine and mature garden. Long ago she had eliminated the old golf course and transformed the grounds of Airlie into an enchanting showplace. She cultivated the multi-acre natural garden at Airlie with the help of Rudolph A. Topel, an accomplished horticulturist. "She liked to joke that she stole Topel from the Kaiser. That's what she told people," said George Evans. He heard her tell the story many times.

The Joneses and Walters, who had met the brother of Kaiser Wilhelm II, Prince Henry, in 1902, got to know the German royal family better in 1903 when they cruised the Mediterranean and were invited to moor alongside yachts belonging to the Kaiser, King Edward VII and Cornelius Vanderbilt, Jr. The Americans accepted an invitation to tour the German palace where Sarah Jones became enamored of Topel's work. She asked the Kaiser's permission for Topel to come to America to work at Airlie. After red tape caused many delays, Mrs. Jones traveled to Germany where she worked a deal with Wilhelm II. "It cost her a lot of money," said Mr. Evans.[115]

Emma and Rudolph Topel, with their daughter, Hilda. (Lois Long Cook)

This is John Henry Rehder and his wife, Johanna, with their four children, (top, left to right) Will, Engelhard, John and (seated) Carl, about 1895. Johanna (1844-1913) is credited with initiating the first long term florist business in N. C. Will and Engelhard Rehder worked together on the grounds of Airlie and Orton Plantation, until Engelhard's death, in 1903. Later, Will created perennial beds and decorated the interior of Airlie for special events. John Rehder, a world traveler, was a frequent guest at the Lodge. Carl Rehder spearheaded Wilmington's Victory Garden program during the Great Depression. (Catherine Marie Gerdes)

Topel provided the expertise, but Sarah Jones Walters had dictated the plan. Determined to follow the natural patterns and materials of nature, for the most part she embellished rather than built and restocked rather than introduced. She transplanted honeysuckle and magnolia from within the garden and added 1200 longleaf pines, 500 live oaks and 5000 camellias.

The lack of exotic transplants mystified at least one helper who turned to ask visiting author E. T. H. Shaffer why anyone in southeastern North Carolina would plant a pine tree. Actually, many of the pines along the mile-long driveway were planted by Mrs. Walters herself, while "kneeling on sacking." She admitted later that she had spaced them fifteen feet apart rather than the recommended thirty.[116]

Local floral authority Will Rehder kept a hand in at Airlie, providing "practical ideas," and greenery and ferns for Airlie parties. But much of the plant material came from "Fruitland," a vast nursery in Augusta, Georgia, owned by the Berckman family. In the 1930s, the Berckmans, nationally noted landscape architects, sold Fruitland to the Augusta National Golf Club, then created the landscaping seen worldwide during the annual Masters Tournament.[117]

As early as 1890, the Berckmans, enterprising gardeners of German descent, sold high quality trees and shrubs to wealthy landowners throughout the South. It is probable that they designed the fairy-tale approach to the Lodge. In the early 1930s, when the Berckmans sold Fruitland, thousands of plants had to be removed to create the golf course. Many came to Wilmington, both to Airlie and to the Frank Beane estate, across Airlie Road. Members of the Berckman family supervised the plantings. The Berckman landscaping at the Beane estate, now removed, was "very old-worldly, like a walk in the Black Forest," but, for the most part, Airlie was fluffy with flowers and open-faced to the sun.[118]

Francis Marion McGowan, the same artisan who made the crosses on St. Andrew's on-the-Sound, built many of the statues in the garden.

"Mrs. Walters had three large, long greenhouses that sat where the parking lot is now," said George Evans, "and they used to have flower beds: rows and rows of flower beds, all different things. All the roads were lined with ivy. This was an amazing place."

Streams - particularly a healthy one, "Church Creek," that crossed Airlie Road near the chapel - were harnessed to create a lake with a mile-long curvaceous perimeter. Two bridges were built and hung with yellow Banksia

The first Airlie bridge was built about 1902. (Airlie Foundation)

roses. Mrs. Walters liked the garden so much she called in an artist to paint on wallpaper upstairs at Airlie House the surrounding azaleas, the lake and its resident black and white swans. Mr. Shaffer, a national authority on gardens, thought Airlie was one that would please even Ruskin, "who saw the perfect garden as a retention of beauty that springs from the divine carelessness of Nature."[119]

"At Airlie is never a straight line, never the slightest hint of artificiality, no obvious seeking after effect, but nature wooed with an understanding heart has responded graciously, revealing here her happiest moods," wrote Mr. Shaffer. John Russell Pope took pride in the garden of his mother-in-law. He admired the subtle Airlie design with its forestlike natural lines and remarked, "If a landscape gardener ever gets inside these gates, he should be shot upon the spot." Tradition holds that Pope procured the iron gates that stand at Airlie's entrance, hand-forged in France and once part of the Vaucluse estate in Newport.

Airlie, about 1895. (Margaret Moore Perdew)

Local children whose parents were friends of the Walterses were invited to the annual Christmas party at Airlie, held a few days before the holiday. Although all the youngsters returned home with expensive and unique gifts, ranging from jeweled watches to miniature Mark Cross tool sets, at least two young Wilmingtonians received extra doses of the Walterses' Christmas spirit. "About a week before the holiday, the Walterses always arrived at Wilmington in their private railroad car and were welcomed warmly. A few days later, they would host the children's party and we went to that as a family. There would be an enormous Christmas tree in the center of the room, with grand ornaments.

Writer E. T. H. Shaffer leans against Airlie's gate, about 1935. Photo by Charles Farrell. (N. C. Division of Archives and History)

"I remember Mrs. Walters very well. She gave the most beautiful parties and sometimes would just invite our family for tea or lunch.But I remember the Christmas parties best. She always gave me something very elaborate, like a white wicker baby carriage with a beautiful doll in it," said Eleanor Wright Beane, daughter of

Eleanor Gilchrist and Thomas H. Wright, and godchild of Pembroke Jones. "One year, she gave me a doll house, large enough for a child to enter. It was fully furnished and had little electric lamps. She gave my brother gifts on the same scale. It wasn't because of anything the two of us did. It was because my father and Pembroke Jones were cousins and very close, and both our parents were such good friends of Mrs. Walters.

Pembroke Jones was best man at the wedding of Thomas H. Wright, pictured here in 1928. I called him "Uncle Tom," said the Joneses' granddaughter, Jane Pope Akers Ridgway. (Eleanor Wright Beane)

"In World War I, Pembroke III was in the Navy. I remember seeing him in his uniform. I had a doll dressed in a sailor suit that his mother gave me for Christmas that year, because dear Pembroke was wearing sailor suits. The doll's body was made of wood and the legs and arms moved. I kept it for a long time."

When Mrs. Walters's granddaughter, Jane Pope, became a teenager, the Christmas night dance became a coveted invitation. "I had a grand time when I went to Airlie," said Wilmington native Rosalie Watters Carr. "Jane Pope's birthday is Christmas Day and they always had a pink party Christmas night, because by the time it was Christmas night, everybody was worn out with reds and greens. Jane was a perfectly nice girl. She didn't put on. They had a goodly crowd down for her party, a group from town and all her family was there, too. I went with Jimmy Carr. Mike Brown was always invited, and Harry Stovall - that group.

Mr. and Mrs. Pembroke Jones III at Sherwood, 1971 (Nancy Sirkis, *Newport: Pleasures and Palaces*)

"Jane's mother, Mrs. John Russell Pope, was a very good friend of Mrs. Sidney Williams, Elliotte Williams, and she might have gotten up the list for Jane's birthday. We'd go there for birthday parties and they would have dinner, a bit formal, but they were warm people. Mr. and Mrs. Pope were there and Mrs. Walters.

"Sometimes I would be invited for tea. They had tea every afternoon so I'd go to Airlie and Mrs. Walters was there. She was fun. She was jolly, just delightful. Jane has said many times that she remembered driving out with 'Grannie' during the day and checking on everything in the yard. She took care of, she watched, everything in the yard. She was very, very particular about the grounds."

Jane Pope Akers Ridgway concurred. "I loved Airlie. I was so happy as the train pulled into the Station at the end of Front Street. However there was no stir or fanfare. Maybe there was when my grandfather was alive. But when I was a girl, we arrived in Wilmington early in the morning and the arrival was quiet and without any incidence. My grandmother and I were very close. She was a wonderful person — affectionate and very unpretentious. Despite having a large staff of employees, she stayed very busy. She planned parties herself and did her share of work.

"I went out with her in the buggy with the buckboard many, many times. It seemed like she inspected every plant, every flower. She took great interest in the help. She would see one of the servants and stop the buggy. 'Hello Tillie, how are you today?'

"Tillie would answer and they would have a short conversation. Then she would drive on to speak to the next servant and the next. She just loved the people who worked at Airlie, just loved them.

"I have my grandmother's dog here in my Rhode Island summer garden. I like to think of her. She was a very affectionate grandmother. We all adored Airlie as did everyone who ever visited there. It was a happy, beautiful, magical place and a great joy to my grandmother who was its creator."[120]

Eleanor Wright Beane remembers attending one of the famous torchlit hunts given in honor of Jane Pope. "They had brought in all kinds of animals. I remember glancing up in a tree and seeing a squirrel wearing a tiny red collar. Others saw it too, but there were so many things to see that no one even commented on it."

"We rode in haywagons and hunted raccoons," said Jane Pope Akers Ridgway. "I was 12 or 13 years old. They were different times."

Though there was much glamour in their lives, Jane Vance London Pope's parents, Sadie and John Russell Pope, experienced great tragedy. The Popes lost their middle daughter, Sarah, at age six, in 1922. In 1931, the same year "Uncle Harry" died, their oldest daughter, Mary, was killed in an automobile wreck, at the age of eighteen. Despite the tragedies, the family continued to visit Airlie on the same metronome-like schedule they had followed for years.

Though Pembroke Jones III inherited the Lodge after his father's death, he preferred living in Newport. Blessed with good looks, but a much quieter personality than his father, Pembroke III played the role of eligible bachelor for years. Finally, at the age of 35, he married Paula Edelen on July 30, 1927. "She was very nice, very good to him," said Eleanor Wright Beane. "She made him happy and managed Sherwood beautifully."

The Walterses returned to the hunting preserve for Thanksgiving and Christmas, and as long as Mrs. Walters lived, the Lodge was maintained. Roland Bradley, a descendant of a Wrightsville Sound slave, chauffeured Mrs. Walters. "Catch that car," she would say if she sighted any of her good friends along the way.

Minnie continued her duties as head housekeeper and Julius and George Evans looked after the grounds and repaired the structural systems. "Just sowing winter rye took a week," said George, in 2001, "and we had to use farm equipment and mules to cut the grass. But then when you stood back and looked at it, that was one beautiful sight."

Henry Walters died in New York, November 30, 1931. His funeral, held at the East 61st Street residence was private. Mr. Walters was buried in a family vault in Green Mount Cemetery, Baltimore. Other Green Mount interments include Enoch Pratt, Sidney Lanier and John Wilkes Booth, who lies in an unmarked grave.

Mrs. Walters opened the Lodge for guests one last time, in December 1938, when Eleanor Gilchrist Wright married William Sterling Roberts Beane III. Mrs. Beane reminisced about her unique honeymoon, 63 years later. "Gracious, the servants were numerous and very attentive and Mrs. Walters had ordered up the largest buffet you've ever seen and left us a very sweet note. The place was hanging in flowers. The main room there was very, very large with great fireplaces at each end, a long center table and lots of tables and chairs around. Dark and plush, not heavier than Victorian but as dark as the Victorian period. That was always my impression of the Lodge: Vastness of size and rather dark."

But after Mrs. Walters's death, in 1943, the future of the house became more fragile. More than a few young Wilmingtonians dared to wander through the moonlit little palace on tiptoe. Many still remember seeing cabinets fully stocked with glasses and wandering through the suites with their distinctive appointments. More sinister visitors came, too, and, over the years, some items vanished. Mount Lebanon Chapel proved to be one of the most charming and vexing features of Airlie for the Walterses. It had been tempting to think of it as their own, since for so long it had sat there, picturesque but mostly unused, in the midst of the Jones-Walters property.

That changed on November 6, 1912, when the Vestry of St. James Church voted to fully reopen the chapel as an outreach for the growing number of year-round Wrightsville Sound residents. St. James was spared most of the price of sprucing up the 77-year-old building, for Pembroke Jones had just seen to all that in preparation for his daughter's wedding there the previous month. The building and 1907 fence were pristine and a brand new pump organ begged to be played. Regular services began immediately and were so popular that worshipers almost needed big shoehorns to squeeze into the straight-back pews. At first, services were held only at night, illuminated by kerosene lanterns and a candle chandelier. Then several communicants from St. James began riding the street car from town to assist with Sunday morning services and to staff a new Sunday School: Thomas Morton, Mary D. Davis, Eloise Burkeimer, Jennie Strange, Mrs. Junius Davis, Annie Kidder, Mr. and Mrs. Anson Alligood, Fannie Grainger and others. By 1920, the Rev. Walter R. Noe was one of the chapel's champions.

Maxine Dizor, a lifelong resident of the Sound, was a young girl at the time and always treasured the memory of Bishop Thomas Darst and Mrs. M. W. Divine paying a visit to her home to invite the Dizors to the "mission" at Mount Lebanon. She was outside playing when they arrived, warmly welcomed but unannounced. "I was afraid to stop and put on my shoes," she wrote many years later. "The Bishop saw me with my trouble, picked me up and put me on his shoulder. With my arm around his neck, I was so afraid I would dirty his coat. But little did he care, for he was truly a man of God." The result of the campaign was so strong that services were held during the week as well as the weekend - and the little chapel overflowed.

Newspaper notices like this one, printed in the *Wilmington Morning Star*, in 1921, kept regular members as well as the curious apprised: "Lebanon Chapel. Wrightsville. Sunday, December 4. Sunday School at 3 o'clock. Evening Prayer and sermon at 4 o'clock. No morning service." Sometimes visitors meandered through the garden to the house and occasionally "boys will be boys" behavior manifested itself in ways Mrs. Walters found objectionable.

In January 1920 Sarah Jones attempted to buy Mount Lebanon Chapel from St. James Church. In 1921, church officials contacted every church in the Diocese of East Carolina in an attempt to obtain information concerning the legal title to Lebanon. The inquiries are curious since a properly recorded deed sat all the while in the courthouse. Perhaps Sarah was under the impression Pembroke Jones had purchased the property.[121]

Nora Dizor and Benjamin Griffith share a moment on the old Airlie bridge, in 1920. (Lossie Griffith Gardell)

Elbow Room

By the time Sarah Jones married Henry Walters, he had retired from many of his railroad duties. Even before World War I, he began to rely on his sister's son, Lyman Delano, a distant relative of President Franklin Roosevelt, who occupied the Emerson-Kenan House on the northeast corner of 17th and Market streets. During the war, the Federal government took over management of the train system. With his enormous need for privacy, the geriatric honeymooners could not handle the stream of Sunday and weekday worshipers. The Wrightsville Sound mission congregation was about to be banished from the garden of Airlie.

Once it became apparent that St. James owned Mount Lebanon, Sarah Walters initiated a drive for a new Episcopal church for Sounders and summer residents. Although she footed most of the bill for the $20,000 church and Mrs. Cornelia Nixon Davis donated land that had belonged to her great-grandfather, William B. Giles, the Rev. Dr. Frank D. Dean did his part as well. A diligent physician turned priest, he carried out the thankless task of soliciting funds for the new building. Maxine Dizor, whose father (William D. Dizor) named the new church after the patron saint of fishermen and Airlie-on-the-Sound, remembered Dr. Dean's campaign. "He would go visit people in their homes and just sit there until they gave a contribution," she said.

St. Andrews on-the-Sound, 1982. (Lossie Gardell)

In 1926, Dr. Dean oversaw the building of the church rectory, now used as a church office. Church members called it the "Deanery." Eventually Dean built a house for himself. A Spanish mission-style house, it still exists, on the southwest side of Bradley Creek. Neighbors began speaking of a story, never substantiated, that Frank Dean quit the practice of medicine after a baby he treated died, from no fault of his own. His training paid off though when St. Andrew's member Nora Dizor Griffith began hemorrhaging. He treated her while they waited for the ambulance.[122]

Dr. Dean also asked Mrs. Walters to open the gardens to the public and to donate the admission charge to the building fund of St. Andrew's on-the-Sound. She readily accepted his idea and proceeded to use her own contacts to boost publicity.

St. Andrew's was dedicated April 27, 1924. The Spanish mission style was probably dictated by Mrs. Walters, who knew that Verrazzano was the first explorer to examine the N. C. coast. Though, according to Colonial scholar Alan Watson, Ph.D., he probably landed just north of New Hanover County, she sought to celebrate his discovery locally. Verrazzano, sometimes a representative of France, hailed from Italy. Mediterranean style was dictated by his granddaughter, Jane Pope Akers Ridgway, in the early 1970s, when she planned to develop Landfall. Asked why, she replied, "to honor the explorer Verrazzano."

Wilmington architect Leslie N. Boney designed the church and U. A. Underwood was the builder. A church member, Airlie craftsman Francis Marion McGowan, built the cross that was hoisted to the roof by men from the congregation. Originally the exterior of the church was brick, but about a year after it was dedicated, stucco was added. Workmen from Pembroke Park paved the parking lot with shells and used a heavy metal disk attached to a long pole to smooth it.

"It is recalled with feelings of awe how the gardens were opened year after year sometime ago, for the benefit of the little church at Wrightsville," stated the *Morning Star*, in 1934. "It is a much loved story of those who know it to believe that these flowers really built this church. The church is too a real little beauty spot and the circumstances of its existence make it more interesting."

The beauty of St. Andrew's on-the-Sound was enhanced by Rudolph A. Topel (1856-1937). Both Airlie's gardener and a member of the church, he was able to channel extraneous materials from Airlie to St. Andrew's, particularly when Airlie Gardens was augmented with materials from the Berckmans' nursery in Augusta. "The grounds surrounding both church and parish house of St. Andrew's Episcopal Church at Bradley's Creek are being beautified by the transplanting of forest trees; maples and other fine specimens of native trees are being removed to the church property."

Henry Walters, (top, 3rd from left), and a crowd at Lebanon Chapel. (St. Andrew's)

As soon as St. Andrew's began to function as a church, Mount Lebanon's double doors closed to the public. In the mid-1930s, E. T. H. Shaffer visited Airlie Gardens and wrote that Mount Lebanon Chapel, "being now within the garden, is used as a private family chapel for the owners, who have however built and endowed another structure outside the grounds for public use."

However, the creation of St. Andrew's Church did not still the tongues of neighbors, some of whom had always felt that Pembroke and Sarah and Henry were a little too influential. After Sarah Walters succeeded in privatizing the chapel, she attempted to deny access to Mount Lebanon Cemetery, a move she thought would help allay recent vandalism. Sometimes the merely curious used Lebanon as an excuse to enter Airlie, then wandered far afield. Flowers and shrubs were destroyed. There was also a history of theft when it came to Airlie's outdoor decorative effects. Two bronze deer prized by Pembroke Jones disappeared, only to turn up, days later, in a Philadelphia junk store.[123]

Doubtless, fear of fire also fueled Mrs. Walters's desire to thwart trespassers. Losing Airlie to fire once and experiencing another blaze at 400 South Front Street was enough to make Sarah Walters deal with possibilities rather than probabilities when it came to such things. Workers installed two outdoor wooden circular staircases at Airlie, customized fire escapes that led from the upper floors to the ground. The fewer people there the fewer likely to drop a burning match or toss a lit cigarette into the dry leaves. Despite all her efforts, there would be another fire at Airlie, in April 1931. Chief Charles Schnibben and the Wilmington Fire Department saved the house, with the exception of three rooms. However, many valuable items were burned or smoke damaged beyond repair. [124]

Despite Mrs. Walters's safety or privacy concerns, those who had family members buried at Lebanon were outraged when she gated them from the cemetery. In their anger they coughed up a litany of neighborhood complaints. In 1889, W. H. Alderman deeded land along Summer Rest Road to the governor of North Carolina for use as an encampment ground. The deed stipulated that if not used for that purpose, the tract would become park property of the City of Wilmington. By 1907, Pembroke Jones controlled the 100-acre site that ran adjacent to Pembroke Park. He placed a high wire fence around the Summer Rest land and blocked off the road. By 1921, a fence surrounded the Airlie property as well.

In 1924, citizens rumbled that his widow had purchased Summer Rest Road property that included the old Encampment Grounds. The sale took place with quiet haste. Local realtors were already busy transforming the parcel, given to the city for the sole purpose of park space, into a "Tourist Camp"when Mrs. Walters learned of their plans. Alarmed, she invited her local attorneys, realtors and a commissioner to Airlie to discuss the situation. Within weeks, commissioners voted to sell the land to Mrs. Walters and the Tourist Camp site was moved to Greenfield Lake.

"The real estate people here are in deadly terror of our losing the Coast Line Railroad if anything is done that she objects to," wrote one angry citizen. "It is an impossibility to persuade our papers that Mrs. Walters is not a public benefactor....I certainly would like to (share) a type-written history of Jones-Walters vs. the Community."[125]

Perhaps Diocese officials winked when Mrs. Walters succeeded in making Mount Lebanon a private chapel and maybe her good works more than made up for the exclusion, but, sixty years later, the neighbors still haven't forgotten it. One former Seagate resident, interviewed in 2001, said "For years, the only way we could get in there was to go to a funeral at Lebanon Cemetery." Eventually, Mrs. Walters reached an agreement with church officials providing ingress and egress for all family members of those interred at Mount Lebanon.

Despite the Walterses' efforts, Airlie still had its vulnerabilities. Young boys like J. Fred Newber, of Seagate, continued to find a way in, if only to take a look around. "By poling a small skiff across the creek and landing in a secluded place along the waterfront, we could sneak onto the grounds and tour the gardens," said Mr. Newber, in 1994. By the late 1920s, there was a lot to look at, for the number of azalea bushes had reached 600,000. During spring, even in moonlight, the blossoms danced with color and the Cape Jessamine (gardenia) flavored the air.[126]

Airlie gardener Jim Ferger and wife, Dora, (top right) pose with other members of the Ferger family. (Christine Leahy, Dora Ferger)

Mrs. Walters made peace with all but a handful and brought pleasure to many thousands of people by opening Airlie to the public in the spring. "The fact that Airlie is the home of Mr. and Mrs. Walters precludes any effort or spirit to commercialize the gardens. It is merely because of the unselfish attitude of the owners that the general public is able to enjoy this marvelous annual floral display," wrote Louis T. Moore.[127]

In 1930, as in subsequent years, Sarah Walters

This bridge still exists at Airlie, but is missing the distinctive upper tier of ironwork. In Mrs. Walters's day, cascades of Lady Banksia roses covered both sides of the span. (Airlie Foundation Archives)

contacted Wilmington Chamber of Commerce Director Louis T. Moore, asking his help in promoting the Spring tour. Moore maintained good relations with a number of press people across three states. It paid off when busloads of journalists arrived at Airlie.

"It is impossible to describe the sight which met the women as they entered the gates!" said writer Rachel Everett. "Masses of Azalea; thousands of them banked along the hillsides and river banks. Perhaps the most impressive scene was the vista which met the view as one turns the road towards the bridge. On the right of the bridge at the bend of the river, a little brook with two waterfalls came tumbling into the large stream; the banks were covered with trees, that with the overhanging moss, grey green willows and masses of ivy made a charming spectacle. The most brilliant masses were on the right. Three kinds of Azaleas were most in evidence. The rich flame color, the pure white and bright rose with a slight bluish tinge were most to be seen. In the background were beds of lupine and softest blue. These, combined with the soft creamy yellow of the clinging roses, made a lovely combination."

Then, interestingly, Ms. Everett added, "Such gardens should be owned by municipal bodies so that every boy and girl could carry this vision of beauty with them through the remainder of their lives. Would it not do more good than art, museums, and picture galleries?"[128]

Actually magenta was the predominant color at Airlie during the Walters era. Deep rose and flame colored azaleas were separated from magenta, often by delicate sprays of white. Blooms cascaded over the edges of the lake, creating the illusion that the plants themselves were underwater. Gardenia abounded, perfuming the entire garden.

Cora Harris, of the *Charlotte Observer,* wrote of the white and purple wisteria, the little violets, and the Old English ivy covering worn marble statues. More than one writer mentioned "Swaying festoons of Spanish moss" and the fact that Airlie-on-the-Sound "was once the old Wright farm." Many visitors were smitten with the miniature house, designed for Mrs. Walters's granddaughters, and Airlie's "romantic bridge," covered in Banksia roses. The bridge exists today, but is missing not only the roses, but also the ironwork, painted white, that ran the length of the span. The graceful white swans still exist: the black swans have disappeared mysteriously.

The Rev. Frank Dean, rector of St Andrew's, helped with all the tours and delighted in pointing out a shaded lane with a 20-foot hedge."I shall show you what all youth the world over loves - Lovers' Lane," he said gleefully. In 1931, the gardens were opened from 8:00 until 6:00, April 24 and 25. Lunch was served by St. Andrew's on-the-Sound, in the Guild Tea Room near the entrance to Airlie. Lunches started at a quarter, but, over time, the price inflated to a dollar and half. Church member Paul Hines caught and supplied fish for the event. Lossie Gardell, so young she had to stand on a crate, washed dishes.

St. Andrew's made an agreement with Tinga nursery to sell azaleas at the luncheon. Average plants were sold for 50 cents, large ones for a dollar. The church and nursery split the proceeds. Visitors from thirty-two states visited the gardens and broke bread at St. Andrew's on-the-Sound.[129]

In 1936, Sarah Walters partnered with friends Annie Gray and J. Laurence Sprunt to give the spring tour. Visitors toured Airlie Gardens and the Sprunts' country residence, Orton Plantation, in Brunswick County. All proceeds went to charity, the majority going to St. Andrew's. Considering that the nation was still in the throes of the Great Depression, the garden tour proceeds were far more overwhelming than they would be today. A single year's take could keep a small church running for several months.[130]

Elsewhere in the Airlie neighborhood things were and had been changing. Heavier automobiles and increased traffic caused the old shell roads to powderize. During dry spells, white dust covered cars and whatever structures were close by. Despite the fact that a lot of the Airlie Road residents liked it fine the way it was — a nice, a pretty oyster shell road, "progress" prevailed. Tarvia, a smooth, odorless waterproof substance concocted from coal tar, had become popular in Newport. In 1916, Pembroke Jones coated and sealed the shell roads that connected his properties in Wilmington with Tarvia. The county followed suit, applying Tarvia to many publicly

Though Airlie Road was used to advertise Tarvia, many residents missed the old shell surface. The boat house on the left became a residence during the Depression and Mamie Jane Fennell's house stood behind the fence on the right.

owned roads.

In 1927, when the Wilmington-Wrightsville Speedway (Oleander Drive) was completed, the Turnpike and many area roads were covered in asphalt. Most Wrightsville Sound residents, already horrified with the change, were appalled when they saw workmen dumping gravel onto the tar. Lossie Griffith Gardell, who lived at Villa View Station, roughly the 7000 block of Wrightsville Avenue, was a girl when it happened, and she and her friends were especially upset because they couldn't skate on the uneven surface. Even the parking lot of St. Andrew's on-the-Sound fell victim to the bumpy addition. Dr. J. Buren Sidbury, founder of Babies' Hospital, understood children: He let them skate on the new parking lot at the hospital while the building was being completed.[131]

By 1926, Giles heirs owned 48 1/2 acres that lay on both sides of Bradley's Creek, assessed that year at $110 per acre. That year the New Hanover County Board of Education purchased 5 acres of the Gileses' land, on the south side of Bradley's Creek, for a school. While Bradley Creek School was under construction, the following letter landed on the editorial desk of the Wilmington Star News. "Right here I wish to say that ... this site is about the worst that could have been chosen. It is covered with dense woods and the school building now being erected is entirely too near the highway, which will make it very dangerous for children and very nerve-wracking for autoists."[132]

Ironically, that same school building now houses the New Hanover County Extension Service, including the Airlie Gardens office. Currently, the "dense woods" contain many outstanding gardens that are known collectively as the New Hanover County Arboretum. The nerve-wracked autoists who puttered their Tin Lizzies down the two-lane "Wilmington-Wrightsville Speedway," built for a cost of $6,000 in the 1920s, would need emotional shock absorbers today if they were to see the volume and velocity of the traffic on Oleander Drive, near Bradley Creek.

Sarah Wharton Green Jones Walters died June 16, 1943, at the Plaza Hotel in New York. She was buried next to Pembroke Jones at Oakdale Cemetery, in a mausoleum designed by John Russell Pope. Sadie Jones Pope, heir to more furnishings than any one person could handle comfortably, decided to sell some of her parents' belongings and hired Wilmingtonian Harry R. Gardner, owner of Murray Transfer, to haul away vans full of treasures from Airlie and the Lodge to New York to be sold at auction by Parke-Bernet Galleries, Inc. There were enough objects — 1456, to be exact — to create a catalogue that filled two hardback books. The inventory included works by Rodin, Peter Paul Rubens, Gilbert Stuart, Sir Anthony Van Dyck and atelier, Jean Antoine Houdon (bust of Voltaire) and Gainsborough Dupont. Additionally, Parke Bernet held separate auctions for Mrs. Walters's collection of French furniture and ormolu, and her books. The sales took place between April 23 and May 3, 1941.[133]

Mrs. Walters also left three horses, two mules, two trucks and five automobiles at Airlie. The cars included a 1932 Ford Phaeton, a 1939 Buick Phaeton, a Buick limousine and a 1941 Buick convertible coupe. The trucks were possibly antiques: Pembroke Jones owned the first chain-driven trucks in Eastern North Carolina.[134]

Mrs. Pope made some changes at Airlie, possibly as the result of storm damage. She removed a heated glass solarium, or garden room, that once was attached to the porte cochere. She also razed the apartments and indoor tennis courts. Sadie Pope, who was frequently in residence at Airlie after her mother's death, had many friends in Wilmington and her stays here were pleasant. She is remembered today as a jolly, easygoing woman, mostly unaffected by the privileges of her birth and marriage.

After 1941, what was left in the Lodge was stolen and the tile floors were hauled away. Particularly senseless, vandals axed and hammered the great stone mantels to rubble and destroyed the beautiful pool on the terrace.

Finally, arsonists destroyed the structure itself, sometime before dawn, in March 1955. A handful of witnesses watched from afar as the great arched windows blazed orange: a Romanesque inferno.

Remnants of the Lodge are scattered across Wilmington, some in living rooms, some in plain view. The two lions that once stood at the gateway were later placed on the steps of City Hall in Wilmington. By 1972, they had been moved to the Kiddie Zoo in Greenfield Park. The balustrade from the Lodge was salvaged after the 1955 fire and added to adjacent homes at 530 and 532 Waynick Boulevard at Wrightsville Beach, now homes of Mimi Burns and Rick Whitford. [135]

In 1982, bulldozers pulverized shards of leaded glass, red tile, and polished stone as they graded Pembroke Park, transforming what had been a recreational retreat to one family into the immense subdivision known now as Landfall. All that remains on the original site are the stark gazebo, scattered rolling coquina terraces and the gates now within the Lion's Gate complex. Pembroke Jones's name remains on the Market Street park he donated, a street and a neighborhood in Landfall and as a town name, Pembroke, N. C., named for Pembroke Jones, a major stockholder in the ACL.

After Harry R. Gardner transported collectibles from Airlie and the Lodge to Parke-Bernet Galleries, there were still many treasures in the house of houses. Sadie Pope called her mother's servants in an distributed most of what was left to them. Tiffany lamps and beautiful jeweled objects made of gold and silver made their way to MacCumber Station and servants' homes on Airlie Road. The Lofton family received framed photographs and an antique bed once owned by Pembroke Jones's father, Capt. Pembroke Jones. Almost as soon as the servants got their treasures home, Wilmington's antique hounds were knocking at the door. To their credit, most of the employees hung on to the Jones-Walters pieces. To their greater credit, they systematically refused to answer questions about their employers' private lives.

Pembroke Jones Park, on Market Street, after McCumber's Ditch overflowed, about 1927. (Cape Fear Museum)

Mr. Corbett Buys a Garden

On November 9, 1947, it was announced that Airlie would be open Nov. 15 through June 30, 1948. "Mrs. John Russell Pope will open Airlie each Sat., Sund. and Mon. from 1-6." However, rumors began around Christmas that Airlie had been sold to Bertha Barefoot and Waddell A. Corbett. The $150,000 deal was sealed January 16, 1948. Two weeks later, the worst ice storm in recorded history hit Wilmington, causing $50,000 damage to the estate.[136]

The Corbett family lived in the Walterses' house in 1949-50. Servants Thelma Mack and Mariah Mandy continued to work at Airlie. "They were wonderful people," said Elsie Corbett Hatch. "They were also faithful people. They never said an unkind word about anyone. They were lovely."

The extended family included parents Bertha and Waddell Corbett, and some of their children: Elsie Corbett and Fred Hatch, Wilbur Corbett, and, on occasion, Jo Corbett and Gilliam Horton. Wilbur Corbett was still recovering from experiences in World War II. He had been wounded and taken prisoner in Germany. Among other horrors, he had emergency hip surgery without benefit of anesthesia. Sometimes he would waken in the wee hours of the morning and he and his brother-in-law, Fred Hatch, would walk the gardens for an hour or two. "Sometimes he wanted to talk about it and sometimes we would just walk in silence. He told me what peace he knew, he found at Airlie," reminisced Mr. Hatch, in 2001.

"What I'll be needing that house for is not known to me," Waddell Corbett had said when he bought it. It became more apparent with time. With 33 rooms, 11 full baths and 20 half-baths, Airlie proved to be too much house

Bertha and W. A. Corbett pose at Airlie, about 1949, with children: Dorothy, Waddell, Elsie, Wilbur, Horace and Josephine. (Albert Corbett)

for him. In 1955, they dismantled it and built their own home. The two sons of Mrs. Corbett's sister, Effie Barefoot Burney, spent a lot of time at Airlie after their cousins took possession. When the old house was dismantled, John J. Burney and his brother, Louis A. Burney, rescued the bar sink and kitchen cabinets. They installed them at their hunting camp in Pender County. Hurricane Floyd destroyed the bar, but the cabinets are still there.

The Corbetts carefully crated a historic carved newel post and rail that had been part of Sir Walter Raleigh's home. It remained in storage for years before being given to a local nonprofit organization. Sadly, a workman mistook the crate for trash and discarded it in a local landfill.

However, the Airlie ballroom survives. Waddell Corbett gave all the material that comprised the ballroom to Airlie butler Charlie Whitty. Mr. Whitty recycled the lumber into "The Barn," a nightclub at 1020 South 11th Street. "Louis Armstrong, Cab Callaway, Ella Fitzgerald: they all performed there," said Charles Fisher, 80, a former railroad chef who was a friend of the Whitty family. "It wasn't a big place and it was so thick in there with people that you could barely see the performers. That was before the days of integration. It was a black nightclub, but whites came, as spectators."[137]

From January to March 1951, the Corbetts planted 5000 azaleas at Airlie, to make up for $50,000 worth of damage due to ice storms in the late 1940s. The storms killed so many trees and shrubs that one observer said Airlie had that "new-haircut" look, a term instantly understandable to anyone who has weathered either a severe ice storm or a hurricane.[138]

"Design: Airlie Garden," is scarce among Minnie Evans's paintings because of its asymmetry.. (Collection American Shaker, Courtesy of Luise Ross Gallery, New York)

"It was just awful," said Elsie Corbett Hatch, one of Waddell's daughters. "I was home from Meredith College and I drove Daddy down there after one of the ice storms. We drove in through Mr. Taylor's gate. We always called him 'Mr. Taylor.' It was the first time I had ever seen Airlie. There were trees down, so much destruction. We lived in a convenient location, on Market Street, and our yard was in good shape. At first, I couldn't understand why Daddy wanted to live so far from town." [139]

Wilmington's most famous photographer, Hugh Morton, shot this photo in 1961. The little girl is his daughter, Katherine Morton. Mr. Morton remembers meeting Sarah and Henry Walters at his grandfather's house, the Hugh MacRae Castle, at 713 Market Street. (Hugh Morton)

Elsie Corbett understood fully when her father's efforts came to fruition. The Corbett plantings included many new species and stretched from the "eagles at the gate" to the Airlie oak, about a half mile away. Gardenias, some rare evergreens and new camellias were added, as well as saplings.

Other than being the site of many Azalea Festival garden parties and innumerable tours, during the 1950s and 60s, the name Airlie snared the attention of a visitor in 1958. The Earl of Airlie, Lord of Cortachy Castle in Angus, Scotland, happened to touch down in Wilmington, at little Bluethenthal Airport. Maybe he had been seated next to a Wilmingtonian, for by the time the plane landed, he knew there was an Airlie in New Hanover County and he knew the name of the greatest living local historian, Louis T. Moore. The Earl phoned him from the airport. Mr. Moore was not home, but the Earl left a message: "Where did the name Airlie Gardens originate?" Mr. Moore wrote him, on March 13,"The name was selected in honor of the Scottish home of the Pembroke Jones ancestors who went from Scotland first to Fauquier County, Virginia."

But mostly, in that era, Airlie was simply home to Bitsy and Waddell Corbett and their children: Albert, Jeannine, Mary Alice, Selah, and Rita. The Corbett family made changes. They replaced the eagles atop Airlie's gates with pineapples, after someone stole one of the birds. They extended the pier, renovated the stables, and added park benches and statuary. Waddell Corbett planted the Corbett Memorial Garden, near the pergola. His children nicknamed it "Waddell Walk."[140]

"Before embarking on other careers in the late-1960s, George Evans's two oldest sons, (left to right) George, Jr. and Norris, worked for subsequent owners, the Waddell Corbett family. When merely boys they helped Julius Evans at Airlie. "We worked with my granddaddy, Papa Julius. He was getting old and we would shift gears on the tractor for him," said Norris, in 2001. (Susan Block)

The Corbett family kept the grounds around it groomed, but lack of use and destructive nocturnal visitors took a great toll on Lebanon Chapel. They ripped windows away from the frames, gouged holes in the doors, destroyed the pulpit, and hammered the 50-year-old organ. They completed their defilement of the little temple by covering the floors and pews with litter and

Lebanon, about 1969. (Lossie Gardell, St. Andrew's on-the-Sound)

excrement. Neither was the cemetery considered sacred: vandals dug up graves, removed ironwork and shrubs, razed plot walls, damaged large tombstones and stole smaller ones.

As the Rev. Herbert Aman pushed for restoration, once again, the Lebanon deed was researched. In 1972, Waddell Corbett gave a substantial contribution toward its restoration and supplied most of the labor and materials. Workmen attempted to recreate the chapel as it was in 1835. They removed two small wings that had been attached to the rear of the building for the Jones-Pope wedding, to protect the bridesmaids from the weather. Local boatbuilder and woodcrafter Julius Herbst created a new altar.[141]

It is possible that the present pews are the third ones to sit in Lebanon. Pembroke Jones, probably about 1912, gave the original Lebanon pews to another church. More pews must have replaced those, because the present pews were made by Airlie superintendent W. A. Taylor for the Parish Hall at St. Andrew's before they were moved to Lebanon.[142]

The Alper family, owners of Queensboro Steel, donated and installed a steel rod to strengthen the structure. Other gifts followed, including generous help from members of St. James Church and St. Andrew's on-the-Sound. St. Andrew's rector, the Rev. Herbert L. Aman, and the Rt. Rev. Thomas Henry Wright, Bishop of East Carolina and a great-grandson of Dr. Thomas Henry Wright, led the committee that pooled the efforts and expertise of many Wilmingtonians, including James C. Fox, Sarah D. Webb, Maxine Dizor, John C. Drewry and Mr. Corbett. Elizabeth Labouisse Wright, wife of businessman and preservationist Thomas H. Wright, Jr., contributed two pre-Raphaelite style stained glass windows that once graced the chapel of her family's plantation, Fairntosh, in Durham County.[143]

During the restoration, the women of St. Andrew's on-the-Sound organized a Lebanon Chapter, dedicated to preserving the chapel. The group still exists and donates annually to Lebanon's preservation. When it came to their attention that repairs were being made to the chapel, two sisters, one in Memphis and one in New York, donated two original alms basins, engraved THW, for Dr. Thomas Henry Wright.

The Rev. Aman and Bishop Wright. (Elaine Henson, Lossie Gardell, St. Andrew's)

When finally Mount Lebanon Chapel was rededicated, in 1974, Bishop Thomas Henry Wright led the service. The service contained a baptism for Allison Ligon Bundy, the first such occasion at the chapel in fifty years. The Rev. Herbert Aman, who had fought so hard for Lebanon's restoration, pleaded with the congregation: "Ask God to take care of this chapel. Ask him in your prayers and you will see, it will be done."

"Although Lebanon Chapel was started by communicants of St. James Church, Wilmington, the indications are that the affiliation of its people and their descendants were, and still are, connected more with St. Andrew's Church, Wrightsville, than with any other Episcopal Parish," wrote Bishop Wright in 1972. The statement was true at the time, but now St. James has taken a more active role.[144]

Although Mount Lebanon Chapel has been electrified, the delicate building has been spared such invasive improvements as central heating and air conditioning. Some concern has been voiced about the central supports, but the cypress trunks have stood for 166 years. Even if new beams do become necessary, Mount Lebanon is still one of the oldest and least altered structures in New Hanover County.

Herbert Topel, son of Rudolph Topel, far left, W. A. (Bud) Taylor (second from right) (Christine Leahy, Lois Cook)

Mrs. Jane Pope Akers, granddaughter of Sarah and Pembroke Jones, took control of Pembroke Park in 1948 under a life estate holding and inherited the tract on the death of her uncle, Pembroke Jones III, in September 1970. With her husband Anthony Akers, a former U. S. Ambassador to New Zealand, she created Landfall Corporation in 1971. They planned a development of large-tract lots that would feature Mediterranean architecture, but after Mr. Akers's death, in 1976, she sold the property to the Goforth Corporation. Mrs. Ridgway remarried several years ago. She and her husband, Tom Ridgway, live in Florida and Newport. Mr. Ridgway, an old friend of the Pope family, is from Philadelphia.

The bronze mastiff, commissioned in Berlin, once stood at the entrance to Henry Walters's 130-acre Baltimore estate, St. Mary's. In 1924, when Mr. Walters sold St. Mary's, the dog found refuge at Airlie. Today, the mastiff is with Jane Pope Akers Ridgway, at Crossways, her Newport residence, the same home once owned by Mrs. Stuyvesant Fish. (Charles Farrell, N. C. Division of Archives and History)

In 1997, following hurricanes Bertha and Fran, the Corbett family decided to sell Airlie Gardens. Though once again there was some confusion as to the dimensions of the Mount Lebanon Chapel tract, real estate brokers proceeded to market the Corbett land at Airlie. However, on January 11, 1999, following many editorials, meetings and negotiations, New Hanover County purchased Airlie Gardens from the Corbett family. Camilla Herlevich, of Coastal Management Trust, played a major role. According to County Manager Allen O'Neal, who assisted with every detail, "Had it not been for Camilla, Airlie would now be just another subdivision." Bobby Greer, Scott Corbett, Albert Corbett, Buzz Birzeniecks,

The house at Airlie was challenging to photographers; it was too large to capture in one picture. Famous N. C. photographer Charles Farrell took this shot in 1935 when he accompanied author E. T. H. Shaffer through the garden. (N. C. Division of Archives and History)

Wanda Copley, Charles Howell, Bill Caster, Ted Davis, and Bruce Williams, Airlie's first director, also did their part to preserve the garden of Wilmington. The present staff includes director Thomas Herrera-Mishler, Wendy Knowles, Gary Rzepecki and Fonda Price. Today, as urban sprawl covers New Hanover County, the preservation of Airlie Gardens is more important than ever. Proverbial green space, punctuated annually with nature's floral fireworks, it provides sustenance for the soul and cleansed air for the body. That it has such a rich history is a fine, fine bonus.

Jane Pope Akers Ridgway poses in her Newport home beneath the childhood portrait of her grandmother, Sarah Green Jones Walters, in 2001. Mrs. Ridgway, known to her close friends as "Popey," is the daughter of Sadie Jones and architect John Russell Pope. (Thomas Ridgway)

Airlie Road, a wonderland of live oak and moss, in 1972 (New Hanover County Public Library)

Footnotes

1 John Lawson, *Gent. Lawson's History of North Carolina*. Richmond, 1957. (Originally published in London, 1714.) Lawrence Lee, *Indian Wars in North Carolina (1663-1763)*. Raleigh, 1963.

2 Deed book AB, page 106, New Hanover County Register of Deeds. Claude Wingate, "Our Little Church." New Orleans, 1858. Map Showing Title to Salt Marshes of Wrightsville Sound, Eric Norden (New Hanover County Public Library). Deed book AB, page 319, NHCROD. Author's interview with Bill Creasy.

3 Land Grant No. 631, State of N. C. LCFHS. Book L, p. 143, NHCROD. E. Lawrence Lee, *The Lower Cape Fear in Colonial Days*. Chapel Hill, 1965. Elizabeth F. McKoy, *Early New Hanover County Records*. Wilmington, 1973.

4 Blackwell P. Robinson, *The Five Royal Governors of North Carolina (1729-1775)*. Raleigh, 1968.

5 Deed book L, page 826. NHCROD. Wright family files, LCFHS. Elizabeth F. McKoy, *Early Wilmington Block by Block*. Wilmington, 1967.

6 DB O, page 290, NHCROD. (The Wright-Bradley sale satisfied conditions of the estate of John Ervin, a former owner of Governor's Point.) Lawson. Eugene Hicks Collection, NHCPL.

7 William B. Giles to Mrs. Giles, June 2, 1857. Newport, Delia Lopez to Eliza Reston, October 31, 1808 ("I hope the pure air has restored him to health and the society...diverted his mind.") Southern Historical Collection, U.N.C. C. Dudley, Jr. to John Scott, August 13, 1825. Lower Cape Fear Historical Society.

8 Psalms 92:12. *The Raleigh News and Observer*, October 21, 1962. "Wrightsville Beach," by Jane Hall. North Carolina

Collection, U.N.C.. Adelaide Meares Papers. Duke University Manuscripts Collection.

[9] Lazarus files, Lower Cape Fear Historical Society. DB Y, p. 528, NHCROD.

[10] Wright Collection. Lower Cape Fear Historical Society

[11] Mount Lebanon insurance documents. Archibald Murphey Collection. NC Archives. LCFHS. Eugene C. Hicks, *Hicks, Ward, Wright, Yonge and 7812 Descendants.* Wilmington, 1982.

[12] Author's interviews with Eleanor Wright Beane, George Kidder and Margaret M. Perdew.

[13] Delia Lopez to Eliza Reston, Newport, October 31, 1808. Giles Collection. SHC.

[14] Giles Collection, SHC. Wright-Dudley-Scott Collection. The Rev. Thomas Wright (1785-1835), August 13, 1825. LCFHS.

[15] Eugene Hicks Collection, NHCPL. Giles Collection, SHC, UNC.

[16] Eleanor Wright Beane Papers. James Sprunt, *Chronicles of the Cape Fear River* (1660-1916). Meares Collection, Duke University Manuscript Collection.

[17] Special Collections. Union College, Schenectady, N. Y. Ellen Davies-Rodgers, *The Great Book*. Memphis, 1973. Scott-Wright correspondence. LCFHS, Catherine W. Bishir, *North Carolina Architecture*. Chapel Hill, 1990.

[18] Giles Collection, William Giles to Mrs. W. B. Giles, July 12, 1870. SHC.

[19] DB M, pg. 571, NHCROD. Emma Woodward MacMillan, *Wilmington's Vanished Homes and Buildings*. Raleigh, 1966. DB M, page 571, NHCROD.

[20] Adelaide Meares Collection, Duke University Manuscripts Collection. Hugh MacRae II Collection.

[21] Transcription of Dr. Wright's handwritten notes, which were kept in the Mount Lebanon Chapel Bible for many years. (Adelaide Meares Collection, DUMC.) James Severin Green (1792-1862), whose family name is incorporated into the name, "Greenfield Lake," was the brother of Mary Hostler Green who married the Rev. Thomas Wright, Dr. Wright's first cousin. Mr. Green lost his life ministering to the sick during Wilmington's yellow fever epidemic.

[22] Interview with Maxine Dizor, 1996.

[23] Adelaide Meares Collection. Duke University Manuscripts Collection. Note: The "little organ" was actually a melodeon that was presented by Dr. William B. Giles. It remained in the chapel until 1912 (about the time when Sarah Jones wed John Russell Pope) when it was returned to Dr. Giles's grandson, Clayton Giles, Jr.

[24] The Reverend R. B. Drane, "An Address Delivered in St. James Church, Wilmington, N. C., at the interment of Dr. Thomas Henry Wright." Wilmington, 1861. North Carolina Collection, Wilson Library, University of North Carolina. Image Archives, Cape Fear Museum. Earliest known photograph of St. James Church, courtesy of Amon Carter Museum, Fort Worth, Texas.

[25] Adelaide Meares Collection, DUMC.

[26] DB CC, p. 287, NHCROD. Giles Collection, SHC, UNC. Author's interview with Lossie Gardell. St. James Church records, LCFHS.

[27] Louis T. Moore, *Stories Old and New of the Cape Fear Region*. Wilmington, 1956. Author's interview with historian Delmas Haskett, 2000. Giles Collection, SHC, UNC.

[28] Wright and Bradley documents, LCFHS. Deed book L, page 656, NHCROD. The Thomas H. Wright, Jr. Collection. Gilbert Cope, *Genealogy of the Sharpless Family*. Philadelphia, 1887. Eric Norden Maps, NHCPL. Anne Russell, *Carolina Yacht Club*

Chronicles. Carolina Yacht Club minutes, LCFHS.

29 *Messenger*, May 1, 1886. Carolina Yacht Club minutes, LCFHS.

30 William B. Giles's drug account with Webb and Dickson, May 16, 1863. Giles Collection, SHC.

31 Giles Collection. Southern Historical Collection, University of North Carolina.

32 Henry Shaw, "A Captured Town." (1895) Special Collections, New Hanover County Public Library. John Johns, "Wilmington During the Blockade." Harper's New Monthly Magazine, 1866. North Carolina Collection, UNC.

33 WB D, page 206, NHCROD. Eleanor Wright Beane Collection.

34 Will Book D, page 206: DBWW, 378 NHCRD. Giles Collection. Southern Historical Collection. University of North Carolina. Anne Russell, *Carolina Yacht Club Chronicles*. Wilmington, 1993. Deed book QQQ, page 730; book 207, page 144, New Hanover County Register of Deeds. Interviews with Eleanor Wright Beane, 2001.

35Wright-Meares-Lovering House, LCFHS. Documentation on 602 Market Street includes a19th-century insurance map and diagram(LCFHS), Reston documents and series of articles published in the *Wilmington Morning Star* noting alterations to the house (Block files, LCFHS.) Carolina Yacht Club minutes, LCFHS. Henry Bacon McKoy, *Wilmington, N. C., Do You Remember When?* Greenville, 1957.

36 Morning Star, "A Tribute from the Wilmington Cemetery Committee." May 21, 1878.

37 *Wilmington Morning Star*, February 5, 1890. Lewis Philip Hall, *Land of the Golden River*. Wilmington, 1975. Accounts by Fred Newber, NHCPL.

38 Bradley documents, Richard Bradley to Henry Savage and Zebulon Latimer, March 3, 1855. LCFHS.

39 Henry Bacon McKoy, *Wilmington, N. C., Do you Remember When?* Greenville, S. C., 1957.

40 DB SSS, p. 684, NHCROD. Hall, LOTGR.

41 Alexander Sprunt Collection, DUMC. Dickinson and Lazarus records, LCFHS.

42 Book TT, page 74. NHCROD

43 Lazarus Collection, J. P. Jones to Mrs. Mauger London, June 2, 1861. LCFHS. Gillie Cary McCabe, *The Story of Old Hampton.*Richmond, 1929.

44 deRosset Collection. Alice deRosset, January 25, 1865. CFM.

45 *Confederate Veteran*. XVIII, p. 533. 1910. New Hanover County Public Library. Ida Brooks Kellam Library files, LCFHS. Transcribed copy of *Journal of John London*, in possession of Kathryn London Stirk, 2001, Winter Park, Fla.

46 Charles M. Andrews, *Colonial Folkways.* New York, 1921. LCFHS.

47 J. C. Chase map, 1892. Courtesy of M. F. Underwood, reprinted in The Island Quarterly (Jay Johnson), Fall, 1999.

48 Latimer family files, LCFHS. `

49 J. S. Reilly, *Wilmington - Past, Present and Future.* Wilmington, 1884. NHCPL.

50 Glenn Hoffman, *A History of the ACL Railroad*. Jacksonville, 1998. Walter E. Campbell, *Across Fortune's Tracks*, Chapel Hill, 1996.

[51] Richard Hunter, Warrenton, Warren County, N. C., Catherine W. Bishir, *North Carolina Architecture*, Chapel Hill, 1990.

[52] Note: The fact that she would later have an audience with the Pope, in 1905, is inconclusive. Wilmington businessman Col. Walker Taylor, a staunch Presbyterian, and Eleanor and Thomas Wright, pillars of St. James Church, also had an audience with the Pope. It's possible that Henry Walters engineered the meeting. His father, William, had strong Catholic leanings after extensive travels in Italy — and probably gave generously to the church.

[53] Christine Leahy's correspondence with Therese Cannone and Mary Adele Griesacker, Notre Dame College of Maryland, Alumni Association and Archives. *Wilmington Dispatch*, March 29, 1905. William S. Powell, ed., Claiborne T. Smith, *Dictionary of North Carolinian Biography*, Vol. 6, p. 121.

[54] William R. Johnston, *William and Henry Walters: The Reticent Collectors*. Baltimore, 1999. *Wilmington Star*, December 6, 1884. William S. Powell, ed., *Dictionary of North Carolinian Biography*, Vol. 2, 362. Christine Leahy's interview with Marie Parker, Fayetteville.

[55] *Fayetteville Observer*, November 11, 1884.

[56] DB WWW, p. 361, NHCROD. Kerchner Records, William Reaves Collection, NHCPL.

[57] New Hanover County Register of Deeds. "History of Mount Lebanon Chapel." (1936) Lower Cape Fear DB YYY, page 35; XXX, 465, NHCROD. Historical Society.

[58] *Princeton Alumni Weekly*, May 16, 1947. Seeley G. Mudd Manuscript Library, Princeton University. Merle Chamberlain, "Latimer Family Compilations." LCFHS.

[59] NHCROD. Latimer family records, LCFHS. Merle Chamberlain, Latimer family researcher. Author's interview with Elsie Corbett and Fred Hatch, 2001.

[60] *Princeton Alumni Weekly*, May 16, 1947.

[61] L'Arioso Files, LCFHS. Leslie N. Boney, Jr., *The Cape Fear Club: 1967-1983*, Wilmington, 1984. Diane Cobb Cashman, *The Centennial History of the Cape Fear Country Club*, Wilmington, 1996. NHCROD.

[62] *Morning Star*, June 17, 1888.

[63] Today the Blockade Runner hotel occupies the Brown Pavilion site.

[64] Wilmington *Messenger*, August 22, 1897. "Residences on Wrightsville Sound." LCFHS.

[65] *Pasadena Daily News*, May 25, 1910. Joelle Gilbert, Angus Archives. Dickinson and Giles family papers, Lower Cape Fear Historical Society.

[66] Bradley documents, Lower Cape Fear Historical Society.

[67] Wilmington *Messenger*, November 28, 1889.

[68] William R. Johnston, *William and Henry Walters: The Reticent Collectors*. Baltimore, 1999.

[69] William R. Johnston, *William and Henry Walters: The Reticent Collectors*. Baltimore, 1999. Leslie N. Boney, Jr., editor, with sketches by James L. Allegood, *Cape Fear Club*. Wilmington, 1984.

[70] Author's interview with Henry J. MacMillan, 1990.

[71] Author's interview with William R. Johnston, 2001; Henry J. MacMillan, 1992.

72 *Morning Star*, February 13, 1890.

73 Block files, LCFHS.

74 Author's interview with James L. Sprunt, Jr., 1999. Alexander Sprunt Collection, DUMC. Reported in the Wilmington *Messenger*, May 27, 1896.

75 Author's interview with Eleanor Wright Beane, 2001.

76 *Wilmington Dispatch*, August 22, 1903.

77 Georgie Hurst Franks, *A Brief History of the Wrightsville Sound Community*. Wilmington, 1997. Author's interviews with Eleanor Wright Beane and Rosalie Watters Carr. Bettie Fennell's interview with Ethel Bernard.

78 Hurst, *Wrightsville Sound.*

79 Author's interview with George Evans. William M. Reaves, *Strength through Struggle*. Wilmington, 1998.

80 "Airlie Gardens," Georgie Hurst Franks, *A Brief History of the Wrightsville Sound Community.* Wilmington, 1997.

81 *Wilmington Evening Post*, January 4, 1947.

82 Parke-Bernet Galleries, Inc. The Mrs. Henry Walters Art Collection, 2 volumes. New York, 1941. Reaves, *Strength through Struggle*. Author's interviews with George Evans. Mary E. Lyons, *Painted Dreams*. Boston, 1996.

83 Author's interview with Thomascenia T. McKoy, 2001. *Encore*, December 8, 1994.

84 Mary E. Lyons, *Painting Dreams*. Boston, 1996.

85 William R. Johnston, *Walters. New York World*, reprinted in the Wilmington *Messenger,* September 12, 1899. William S. Powell, *Dictionary of N. C. Biography*, Chapel Hill, 1988.

86 William R. Johnston.

87 Wilmington *Star*, January 10, 1901; February 23, 1901.

88 Land acquisition maps, McKoy Collection. CFM. New Hanover County Register of Deeds. Abstracts by Elizabeth F. McKoy, LCFHS, NHCPL.

89 Dispatch, June 4, 1905. Author's interviews with Eleanor Wright Beane. *Wilmington Messenger*, December 11, 1902.

90 Wilmington *Messenger*, January 21, 1902; February 9, 1902; February 20, 1902, *Wilmington Dispatch*, February 22, 1902. (Note: The Atlantic Coast LIne had its own carpentry shops for everything from office furniture to wooden train cars. Many accomplished ACL craftsmen performed carpentry feats at Airlie.)

91 *Wilmington Home Magazine*. n.d.

92 Louis T. Moore Collection, New Hanover County Public Library. Author's interviews with Mr. Moore's daughters, Florence M. Dunn and Margaret M. Perdew.

93 Plat maps, McKoy Collection. CFM. Samuel Howe, *American Country Houses of Today*. New York, 1915.

94 Will Molineux, "The Memory of a Little Girl and Williamsburg's Restoration." Colonial Williamsburg, Spring, 2001. Various biographical articles published by Mr. Molineux. *New York Times*, March 26, 1913; *Richmond Times-Dispatch*, November 23, 1925; *New York Times*, November 23, 1925.

[95] Author's interviews with George Evans, William Dobo, Luther Rogers, Mary Wilson McCarl. Diane Cobb Cashman, *Cape Fear Adventure.* Woodland Hills, California, 1982.

[96] Steven McLeod Bedford, *John Russell Pope, Architect of Empire*. 1998. Author's interview with Steven Bedford.

[97] Samuel Howe, "American Country Houses of Today." New York, 1915. CFM.

[98] Lewis Philip Hall, *Land of the Golden River.* Wilmington, 1980.

[99] *Morning Star*, October 22, 1909. Records of the Vanderbilt Museum, Centerport, NY.

[100] Author's interview with Robert Bridgers, 2001.

[101] Author's interview with Margaret Moore Perdew, 2000.

[102] *Wilmington Morning Star*, Dec. 24, 1907. 1909. *Wilmington Dispatch*, April 27, 1907. William R. Johnston, *William and Henry Walters: The Reticent Collectors*. Baltimore, 1999.

[103] E. T. H. Shaffer. *Carolina Gardens*. New York, 1937. Samuel Howe, "The North Carolina Estate of Mr. Pembroke Jones." Cape Fear Museum Archives. (Note: In 1915, Mr. Howe wrote of the acreage that would become Landfall, "The place is neither spoiled nor belittled by foolish subdivisions.") Author's interview with Elsie Corbett and Fred Hatch.

[104] Philip P. Masterson Company, Airlie Inventory (Elsie Corbett and Fred Hatch). Author's interviews with Elsie and Fred Hatch, 2001.

[105] Masterson Inventory (Elsie Corbett and Fred Hatch). *New York Times*, October 26, 2001, (Holland Cotter.)

[106]Masterson Inventory.

[107] Ibid.

[108] *The Daily Princetonian*, January 4, 1907, Princeton University, Seeley G. Mudd Manuscript Library. Author's interview with Kenneth M. Sprunt, 2001.

[109] According to Jane Pope Akers Ridgway, except to very close friends, her grandmother was called "Sarah"; her mother, "Sadie." *Wilmington Evening Post*, January 4, 1947.

[110] "Leading Society Folks Wed Near Wilmington." Lower Cape Fear Historical Society.

[111] Anne Garside, *The Johns Hopkins Peabody News Online*: Interviews with William Johnston, Walters Art Gallery.

[112] William R. Johnston, *William and Henry Walters.*

[113] Leora Hiatt McEachern, *History of St. James Parish, 1729-1979.* Wilmington, 1982.

[114] William Johnston, *The Reticent Collectors: William and Henry Walters.* Baltimore, 1999. Author's interview with George Evans, 1999.

[115] Author's interview with George Evans, 2001.

[116] Ibid. Walter E. Campbell, *Across Fortune's Tracks*. Shaffer, *Carolina Gardens*.

[117] *Wilmington Morning Star*, April 19, 1931.

[118] Eleanor Wright Beane Collection.

[119] NHCROD. Shaffer, *Carolina Gardens*.

[120] Author's interviews with Jane Pope Akers Ridgway, 2001.

[121] Joyner Library, East Carolina University. Martha Elmore, archivist. St. James Records, courtesy of Edward F. Turberg.

[122] Interviews with Lossie Griffith Gardell, 1996-2001. (Note: Mrs. Gardell said that Rudolph Topel told her grandfather, William Dizor, that Dizor was a shortened form of the German surname, Van Dizor.)

[123] *Wilmington Morning Star*, February 14, 1917; February 16, 1917.

[124] *State* magazine, February 29, 1936 (Susan Iden.) Author's interviews with various Airlie neighbors.

[125] Mary D. Cronly to B. D. MacNeill, October 9, 1924. NHCPL.

[126] *Encore* magazine, December 8, 1994.

[127] *News and Observer*, April 19, 1931.

[128] Reprinted in *Wilmington Morning Star*, April 21, 1931. *Charlotte Observer*, April 27, 1930.

[129] Author's interviews with Maxine Dizor and Lossie Gardell

[130] *State* magazine, April 11, 1936.

[131] Louis T. Moore collection, NHCPL, LCFHS. Interviews with Lossie Griffith Gardell, 2001.

[132] *Wilmington Morning Star*, September 23, 1926.

[133] Powell, *Dictionary of N. C. Biography.* Author's interview with Mrs. Luther Rogers, 2001. Elsie and Fred Hatch, Walters's inventory.

[134] Walters's inventory, Elsie and Fred Hatch. Author's interview with James Lofton, 2001.

[135] *Wilmington Morning Star*, November 12, 1972.

[136] *Wilmington Morning Star*, November 9, 1947; December 28, 1947; January 17, 1948; February 3, 1948. Author's interviews with Elsie and Fred Hatch, 2001. Bart Smythe, 1998. NYS DB 982, p. 784.

[137] *Wilmington Morning Star*, April 7, 1955, May 25, 1985.

[138] *Wilmington Morning Star*, April 2, 1951.

[139] Author's interview with Elsie Corbett Hatch, 2001.

[140] Christine Leahy's interviews with Albert Corbett and Jeannine Corbett Squires.

[141] *Wilmington Morning Star*, April 7, 1973; August 11, 1973.

[142] Author's interview with Carl McGowan, 1995.

[143] *Wilmington Morning Star*, March 3, 1974. Author's interview with the Rt. Rev. Thomas H. Wright, 1992. Maxine Dizor, "A Little Girl's Memories," and Lebanon Papers, St. Andrew's on-the-Sound Archives. Interviews with Maxine Dizor, 1996. *Wilmington*

Morning Star, April 27, 1974.

[144] St. Andrew's on-the-Sound Archives.

Johanna Rehder and Tabitha Hutaff at Pembroke Park, about 1927. (Tabitha Hutaff McEachern)

Often, Southern hospitality is manifested in seafood specialties at the table. Here are a few local favorites.

Clam Chowder

Enough clams for 2 cups
2 cups diced potatoes
1/2 cup minced onions
1/2 cup finely diced celery
4 tablespoons butter
1 cup milk
2 cups clam juice
Salt and pepper to taste
1 cup tomatoes

Wash and steam clams until they open. Save juices, and add enough water to cook tender. Drain and chop clams fine. Save water. Add vegetables to water, and cook until tender. Add clams, salt, and pepper. When all are done, add cup of warm milk. Let boil. Serve.

—Virginia Bellamy Ruffin (Favorite Recipes of the Lower Cape Fear, 1955)

Johnnie Cakes

2 cups flour
1/2 cup vegetable oil
1 1/2 teaspoon salt
1/4 cup water

Mix and roll out between wax paper. Place dough on cookie sheet and cut into squares. Bake at 375 degrees about ten minutes.

—Gibbs Holmes Willard (Cape Fear: Still Cooking, 1969)

Edge Hill Crab Cakes

1/2 cup milk
1 pound crab meat
1 slightly beaten egg
1 teaspoon dry mustard
2 teaspoons mayonnaise
1/8 teaspoon pepper
1 teaspoon Worcestershire sauce
1 teaspoon Angostura bitters
1 teaspoon chopped parsley
1 teaspoon salt

Make into cakes. Dip in milk and then in cracker crumbs. Place on baking sheet in 375 degree oven for 20 minutes. Serve with Caper Sauce.

Caper Sauce

1 1/2 cups chicken broth
1 tablespoon butter
1 tablespoon flour
1/2 teaspoon salt
1/2 cup capers

Melt butter. Add flour and broth slowly. Add salt and capers.
—Jane MacMillan Rhett (Favorite Recipes of the Lower Cape Fear, 1955)

Roasting Oysters

Dig a 1' deep pit about 3-4 square feet.
Put some bricks around it to prop up a sheet of metal.
Build a fire in the pit and place the metal plate on top.
Put a bushel of freshly washed oysters on the metal plate and cover with a burlap sack,
hose sack to create steam. Oysters are ready when shells part slightly.
Serve with a catsup, horseradish, tabasco and lemon sauce (mix to your taste).
Some folks like melted butter and lemon plus soda crackers on the side.
—Jane Lawton Baldridge

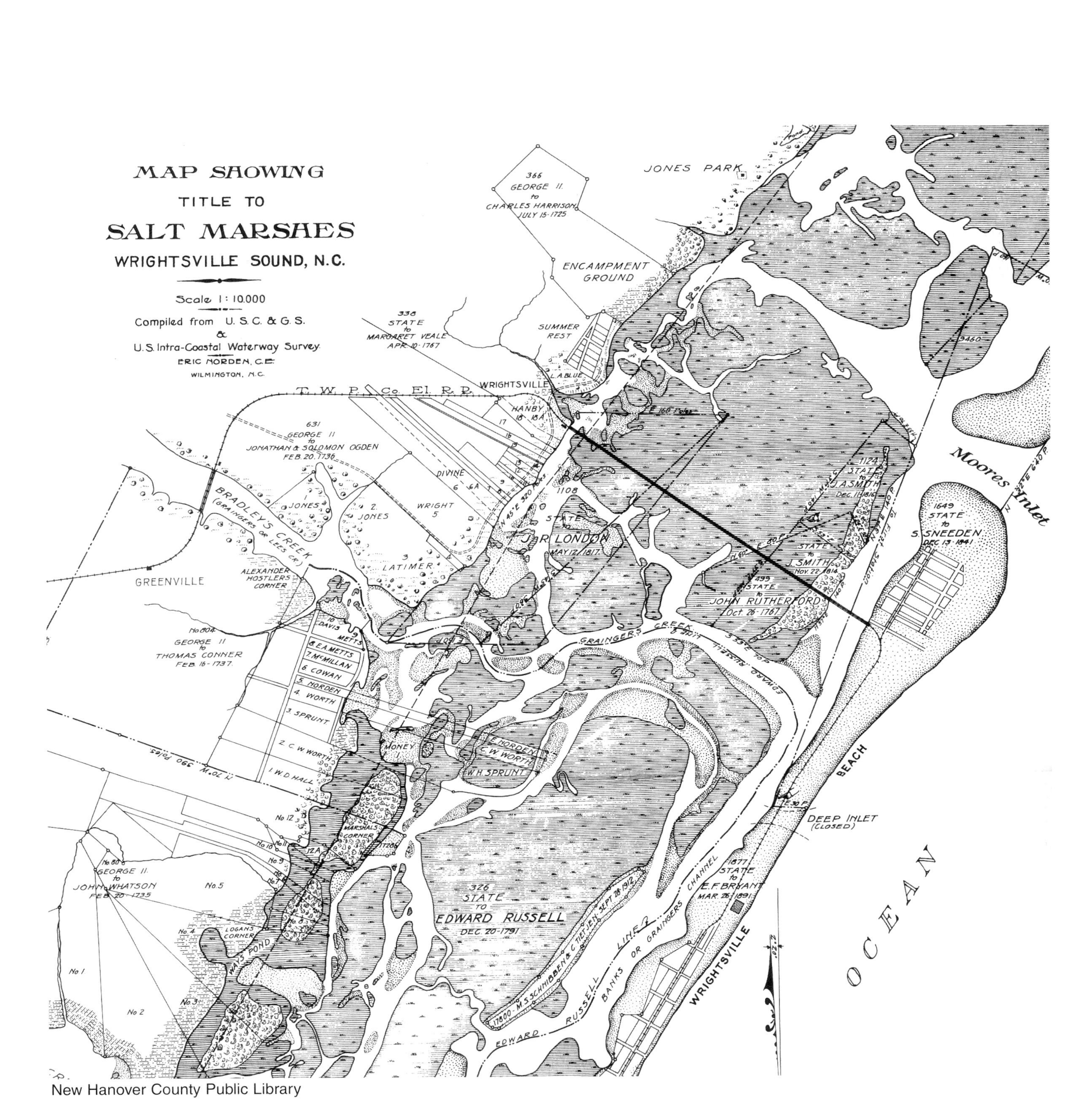

New Hanover County Public Library

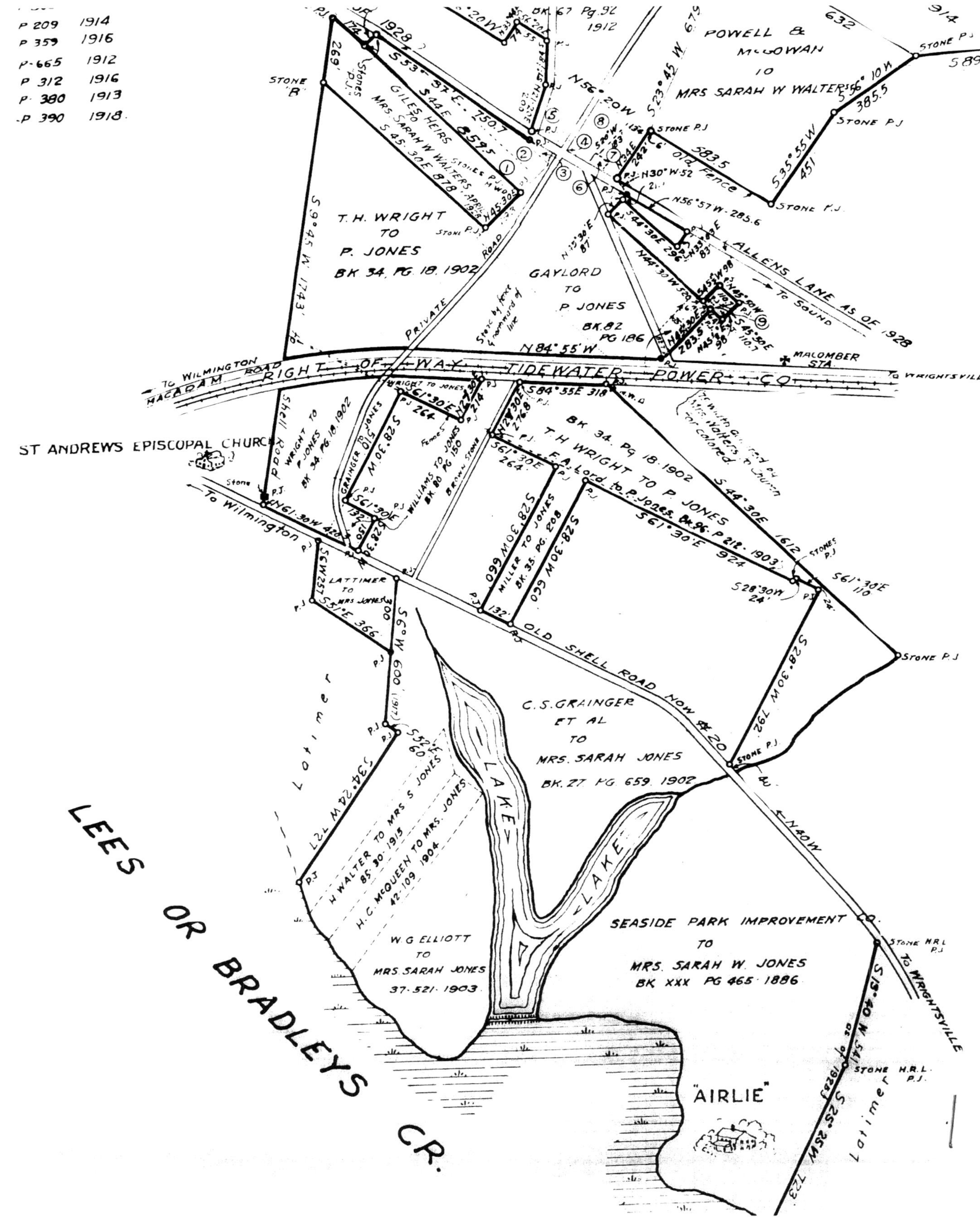

(Cape Fear Museum)

THE STATE
A Weekly Survey of North Carolina
JULY 28, 1945
TEN CENTS

(Lower Cape Fear Historical Society)

Photo by Hugh Morton.

Index

Photo by Jack Davis.

Photo by Jack Davis.

Photo by Jack Davis.

Photo by Jack Davis.

So long! Members of the Meares family are chauffered home from a party at Pembroke Park, about 1912. Sometimes the Joneses leased as many as 20 extra automobiles for their parties. (Lower Cape Fear Historical Society)